A

PERSIA

Persia

BY

RICHARD N. FRYE

SCHOCKEN BOOKS · NEW YORK

Originally published under the title *Iran*, 1960

This revised edition
Published in U.S.A. in 1969
by Schocken Books Inc.
67 Park Avenue, New York, N.Y. 10016

Library of Congress Catalog Card No. 69-14541

PRINTED IN GREAT BRITAIN

Think in this batter'd Caravanserai,
Whose Portals are alternate Night and Day.
How Sultán after Sultán with his Pomp
Abode his destined Hour, and went his way.

Fitzgerald, the best interpreter of Khayyam

Preface

Some people may deplore the frequent references to the past in any discussion about Iran, including the future of the country. But the past weighs heavily upon the population and it is my belief that one cannot ignore the fascinating and glorious heritage of almost three millennia, for that heritage has formed the land and people of today, so much so that even modern, economic development by foreigners can hardly succeed without a knowledge by them of the mores and temper of those to be served by that development. This is why an historical survey of Iran occupies so much of this book. I have sought to temper the list of details by some analysis, but especially by the division of chapters, not by chronology but by topic. One cannot hope to convey more than an impression of the richness of the culture of Iran in a few pages, but this unworthy morsel, to use traditional Persian language, may tempt the appetite to greater adventures.

The broad perspectives of the past can indeed help one to better understand the pressing problems of the moment, and the details of contemporary events can acquire new meaning when placed against the tableau of the history of Iran. I hope this brief survey of Iran's past will provide just a small measure of that background so necessary for our understanding of the present.

NB—The transcription of foreign words is simplified without diacritical marks. It varies, however, as Arabic—Muhammad and Persian—Mohammed.

Richard N. Frye
Aga Khan Professor of Iranian
Harvard University

Contents

PREFACE   *page*   9

    I   Deserts and Mirages   13

   II   The Charisma of the King of Kings   23

  III   Cultural Syncretism   36

  IV   The Flowering of Literature   44

   V   Dualism in Faith   53

  VI   Half the World is Isfahan   63

 VII   The Overdeveloped Occident   73

VIII   The End of an Epoch   90

  IX   The New Iran   105

APPENDIX

   I: Selected Figures in the Development of Iran   118

  II: Chronology of Important Events   119

 III: The National Dynasties of Iran   121

BIBLIOGRAPHY   124

INDEX   126

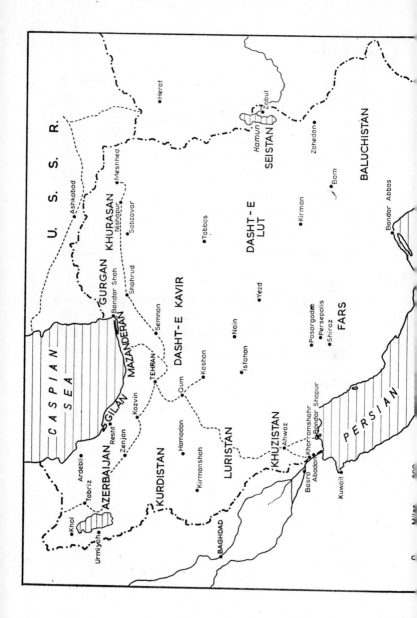

CHAPTER I

Deserts and Mirages

IRAN means the land of the Aryans, what the Greeks and then the West called Persia. As is frequent in foreign designations of a land or country, the Greeks took the name from Persis, the southwestern province whence sprang their contemporaries the dynasty of the Achaemenids. Today, in English, in other European languages, and in this booklet, the two words 'Persia' and 'Iran' are synonymous, while the latter is the sole indigenous designation. In certain scholarly circles, however, a distinction is made between the two; 'Persia' is the present country with the political boundaries it has had for more than a century, and 'Iran' covers the large territory which in the past was Iranian in speech and culture. This 'greater Iran' included and still includes part of the Caucasus Mountains, Central Asia, Afghanistan and Iraq; for Kurds, Baluchis, Afghans, Tajiks, Ossetes, and other smaller groups are Iranians. Pan-Iranian political aspirations have never been strong anywhere but a cultural solidarity is surely real among many of the Iranian peoples. While in this book we shall be concerned only with the modern state of Persia, or Iran, we should not forget that 'greater Iran', which has been important in understanding the primary division between east and west in Persia throughout history.

The two salt deserts, the Dasht-i Kavir and the Dash-i Lut, in the centre of the country, effectively divide it into an eastern and a western part. The eastern provinces of Khurasan and Seistan in dialect and in local customs and usages have, or perhaps had, more in common with Herat province of

Afghanistan than with Fars and Azerbaijan provinces of their own land. The histories of eastern and western Iran too have been different, though the centre of power and of rule in a united country has been invariably in western Iran.

Although the two deserts are in the centre of the plateau, and are the basins for streams descending from the Elburz and Zagros mountain ranges, most of Iran is really a desert with life flourishing in oases, some of them of very large size. Our word 'paradise' came from Persia, and it was originally a private hunting preserve of the Achaemenid king of kings. In a sense every oasis in Iran is a green paradise compared with the surrounding wasteland, and the lovely gardens within are usually separated sharply from the outside world by high mud walls. Most of the cities of Iran lie in oases and the key to life for all is water. Indeed water is the lifeblood of most of the continent of Asia, and on the Iranian Plateau the need for it is always acute. Roads patiently built in the summer or autumn are washed away in the winter or spring by flash floods, and more quarrels arise over the distribution of water than any other factor.

Another feature of the geography of Iran is the barren mountain, for rarely in the country does one lose sight of rugged peaks or hills. The mountains even more than the deserts have kept the Persians so divided that even today there is a multitude of dialects and different customs from village to village. Unlike the huge neighbour to the north where the spoken language is quite uniform from Leningrad to Vladivostok, Iran has diversity to an extraordinary degree. Outside observers have noted that the sometimes harmful individuality of the Persians is a reflection of the rugged physical landscape where they live, and environment surely has had a strong influence on the inhabitant of the plateau.

We have several times spoken of the Iranian Plateau, but one must not forget the two lowland areas not on the plateau which are very different from the plateau yet included within the political boundaries of Iran. The narrow coastline of Gilan and Mazanderan between the Caspian Sea and the Elburz Mountains is below sea level and tropical, a veritable jungle as the Persians call it, where silk, tobacco, and rice are grown. Once ravaged by malaria, the inhabitants of this area, thanks to extensive preventive measures, are now able to live a better life. Many are in stature smaller and darker than the average plateau dweller and they speak several distinctive dialects. Caviar and fishing are important industries here.

The other lowland area, the southwest province of Khuzistan, is really an extension of the plains of Mesopotamia into Iran. Here most of the local population speaks Arabic and the intense summer heat is comparable to that of neighbouring Iraq. The important oil fields and the great Abadan oil refinery rescue the province from being a possible depressed area. On the other hand, the land is fertile and rivers provide necessary water although dams and extensive irrigation canals are necessary for its distribution.

The ethnic map of Iran is not just composed of Persians of various dialects and hue, and of Arabs in the south, but it is much more variegated and mixed. Here again geography has played an important role, and one may speak of certain 'refuge areas' where in the past tribes, religious sects, or political fugitives have fled to escape persecution or attack.

In the southeast is the barren province of Baluchistan where perhaps several hundred thousand Baluchi tribesmen live and where Iran's only active volcano, Koh-i Taftan, is located. The Baluchis speak a language related to modern Persian and they are immigrants from northern Iran to the land which bears their name, probably moving there in the eleventh and twelfth centuries. Somewhat isolated from the rest of Iran, the Baluchis live in a tribal system with a minimum of central government control. The Baluchis extend far into Pakistan and even into Afghanistan, while their way of life is little touched by European civilization. For the most part they are Sunni Muslims, unlike the Persians who are Shiites, and this has been at times one source of friction between the two peoples.[1] Until the time of Reza Shah the Baluchis regularly sent raiding expeditions far into the heart of Iran almost to the gates of Tehran, but at present they use their guns mainly for hunting.

The Kurds in western Iran represent perhaps a third of the entire Kurdish population, the rest being in Turkey and Iraq. The total number of Kurds is unknown but a rough guess of a total of five million might not be far wrong. The Kurds too, for the most part, are Sunnis, but there is little religious friction between them and the Shiites in Iran. The early history of the Kurds is little known but their habitats in the rugged Zagros mountains have been and are areas of refuge from Persian central government control. While the Kurds frequently have played important roles in the history of Iran their tribal organization and loyalties have hindered Kurdish unity and co-operation among themselves or with Persians. Their near relatives to the south, the Lurs, are even less amenable to outside control or influences although the most famous of their tribes, the Bakhtiyaris, have at times exercised great influence on governmental policy in the twentieth century.

The Arab farmers and tribesmen in Khuzistan are not significant in the government or economy of modern Iran, and they have not enjoyed special prestige because they spoke the language of Muhammad the prophet. On the contrary, relations between the Persians and Arabs, though not hostile, can hardly be called cordial. The Shiite holy cities of Kerbela and Nejef are in Iraq and many pilgrims from Iran may be found in the two cities. In history the lowland of Mesopotamia has been frequently under Persian rule though not for the past three centuries. A few ultra-nationalistic Persians consider Iraq as an Iranian *irredenta,* since the Achaemenids, Parthians, and Sasanians ruled there, but on the whole there is little mutual interest or contact between the two peoples.

The largest minority group in Iran are the Turks, probably

[1] On the differences between Sunnis and Shiites, see p. 58.

some four million of them. The major portion of the Turks live in the rich agricultural province of Azerbaijan. The wave of Turkish immigrants from Central Asia in the twelfth and thirteenth centuries transformed Azerbaijan from an Iranian into a Turkish land. To the south in Fars province the closely related Turkish Qashgai tribesmen are the most powerful nomads of the province while eastward in Kirman Afshar Turkish tribes may be found. In the northeast province of Khurasan live Turkomen tribesmen with relatives across the border in the Soviet Union. So Turks are found in most parts of the country.

In a real sense Iran since the sixteenth century has been almost a dual monarchy, ruled by Turks as well as Persians. The shahs of Iran were in origin mostly Turks and the Turks are today an energetic, progressive segment of the population. In the past, attempts of their kinsmen in Turkey to establish close relations with the Turks of Iranian Azerbaijan, called Azeris, have not been successful since the Azeris are primarily Shiites while the majority of Turks in Turkey are Sunnis. Furthermore, cultural differences between the two are strong, and little reason for co-operation existed in the past. More recently, in World War II, contacts with brethren in Soviet Azerbaijan likewise were not overly cordial since the Persian Azeris are committed to Iranian culture and consider their destiny to be with the Persians rather than with other Turks. Indeed it is the culture of Iran which provides the great solidarity complex for the various ethnic groups in the country and many members of minority groups can be more royalist than the shah in proclaiming their devotion to the poetry, the art, and the mores of the Persians. Therefore, in spite of the great number of minorities and the strong provincialism, there is a loyalty to the concept or the charisma of 'Iran' which is difficult to measure but nonetheless real.

Iran frequently has been compared with France and the parallels are many and striking, yet they also can be misleading. For example, the French are said to be pleasure loving, artistic, and even conservatively religious, yet with a strong strain of pessimism in them. They were also considered less martial than their German neighbours, like the Persians *vis-à-vis* the Turks. These are at best generalizations with many exceptions but they do at least serve to stimulate the imagination and provide material for reflection. In another matter, the ability to survive even under foreign or tyrannical native rule, the Persians have been compared to many people who maintain their beliefs and identity even under Communist rule. The Shiite doctrine of *taqiyeh* or *kitman,* perhaps best interpreted as 'dissimulation', has enabled the Persian to escape persecution or even annihilation by not only concealing his true beliefs but outwardly supporting those of the rulers or more powerful neighbours. In other words, the thesis that the end justifies the means was practised in Iran long before Lenin. Here again we have a generalization, and it is a moot point just how much dissimulation dominates the life of the Persian today.

To return to the 'solidarity complex' of the Persians, or their *'asabiyyah,* as the Arab sociologist Ibn Khaldun called it, we may briefly summarize the factors which make a Persian distinct from his neighbours. First, and perhaps most important, is his language and literature. There is no people so addicted to poetry as the Persians, and that includes their businessmen and even peasants. Poetry is far more to the Persian than cuisine is to the Frenchman, rugby to the English, and baseball to the Americans. The verses of Firdosi, Sa 'di, Hafez, and countless others are recited everywhere by everyone. 'Persian [the language] is sugar' goes a phrase which is well known in Iran, and the people love their language. Second, Persian art and crafts though less ubiquitous are a very important expression of the culture of the people. Persian rugs are not made just for export for the Swiss or American markets, but for rug lovers at home, while glazed tilework, wood carving and other arts are treasured by connoisseurs in Tehran as well as abroad.

The richness of Persian culture, as we have mentioned, has an effect on minorities within the country as well as on neighbours and foreigners, similar perhaps to the impact of French culture on western Europe two centuries ago. To venture a surmise, it may be the penetration of this culture to all strata of society, rather than only in a small upper élite which gives Persia a distinctive place in the Near East. This particularity is especially true in general culture but it obtains even in religion.

Iran is part of the Islamic world yet it is a special, distinctive part. Muslims everywhere may be divided generally into the Sunnis, usually called orthodox, and the Shiites, but only in Iran are the latter a dominant majority. Shiism has become the Iranian religion *par excellence,* and it has absorbed many local Iranian features in the course of history. By origin, of course, it was an Arab movement but it became identified with Iran especially after the sixteenth century when the state religion of the land became Shiism.

In most general terms the Shiites stand in the same relation to the Sunnis as Christians to Jews. The messianic, the pathetic, and the 'suffering' features of religion are prominent in Shiism as is legalism in Sunni Islam. But generalities about religion can be especially misleading in Iran for the reputedly strong individualism of the Persians is also manifest in this area. Throughout the history of Iran, both pre-Islamic and later, the ability of the Persian to accept, synthesize and to transform outside influences has been noted by many writers beginning with Herodotus.

The Achaemenid kings, we know, paid homage to the deities of conquered peoples, as in Babylonia and in Egypt, while they were ever willing to learn from their many subjects. The Sasanians, too, borrowed from others in their art and culture, as did later Persians from the Arabs. Today the Persians continue the old tradition by taking over ideas from the West with alacrity. Yet always the Persians have integrated borrowings with their own culture and this has served to stimulate creativity among the people with generally happy results. The readiness to listen to the foreigner is a quality which might be designated the 'ecumenical' urge in the politics and culture of Iran, characterized by tolerance and adaptability. This, of course, was most prominent when Iran was strong and ruling others, but it can be detected at all times.

Even in the realm of religion one might discover this 'ecumenical' propensity or the tendency to absorb and adapt outside ideas. The most famous examples of such religions which developed in Iran, although their roots were in Mesopotamia and Arabia respectively, were Manichaeism in the third century and Bahaism in the nineteenth. Both religions were surprisingly amenable to the incorporation of various ideas and beliefs found in the contemporary religions into their own new faiths. While it would be hazardous to equate this tolerance or adaptability with the belief that all religions are one, and that all should be brought together, nonetheless, I know of few other religions in history which have approached this position more closely than Manichaeism and Bahaism. Again this generalization needs qualification since even the history of Manichaeism is neither consistent nor peculiarly Iranian, but the remark may stand in a wide context.

At the same time, one should not forget the opposite tendency which has been prominent at various times in Iran's history. Fanaticism, the rejection of anything foreign, and withdrawal, a strong exclusiveness, and even cruelty in defending the status quo against reformers and liberals have been manifest many times in Iran's past. The history of the Zoroastrian church is a good example of the restrictive, exclusive features in Persian culture. At the end of the Sasanian empire and under early Islam, the Zoroastrians had a 'ghetto mentality', maintaining an ethnic purity by next-of-kin marriages, with elaborate purification rites and the like. Concern with orthodoxy and heresy was much stronger at that time than it had been previously. One might point out the historical reasons for the change but we are here concerned only with the difference itself. The Shiite state church of the Safavids too became intolerant and opposed other Muslims with a similar exclusive mentality. One might argue, of course, in a Toynbeean or Spenglerian fashion, that all societies have their fluctuations, and that civilizations like people have many facets, some of which come to the fore at one time, others at another. But with the Persians, their extremes have impressed the outsider like the sharp contrasts in colour in that sunny land. If one dared to generalize, he might characterize the Persians as more variable, or unkindly put, as more unstable than their neighbours the Turks or the Arabs. In any case the important point to remember is that they are different from their neighbours in many respects.

Another way of describing this ambivalence in Iranian character might be as a superiority-inferiority complex or in the same breath arrogance and humility. In the nineteenth century many Europeans in Iran were struck by a kind of 'dream world' of the Persians, where a Chinese wall mentality, making Iran the centre of the universe and the shahinshah the greatest monarch in the world, varied with a kind of humility or abject denigration of the character of the individual or his society. This contrast, or 'yes and again no' character, may be found even today, as a Persian nationalist who boasted of his country as a great world power on one side and then remarked on the other that England had given the concept of law to the world, Germany the sense of scientific order and scholarship, while Iran had given the art of lying.

Iran has been ruled by foreigners many times but it has in the end conquered its conquerors. Better a tyrannical Persian shah than a benevolent foreign ruler, say the Persians. Often in Persian history native customs, beliefs and loyalties have been maintained against foreign rule under the guise of the end justifying the means. Yet often the means has become the end, and one tyranny has replaced another. One calls to mind the answer of the Spartans, found in Herodotus, to a satrap of the Achaemenian king who urged them to accept service with the Persians. 'Hydarnes, the counsels which you give us are short sighted. You know only that which you recommend, not that which you urge us to leave. You understand how to be a slave, but you know nothing of freedom. If you had but tasted it you would counsel us to fight for it not only with spears but with axes'.

CHAPTER II

The Charisma of the King of Kings

In the United States the Declaration of Independence and the Constitution have become almost sacred symbols of America. In France it is what Charles Péguy called *la mystique republicaine*. In Iran the counterpart would be the charisma of the shahinshah. In ancient pre-Islamic times this charisma was expressed by a word *khvarnah* or later *farn* 'kingly glory'. While the Persian great kings in Achaemenid and Sasanian times were not actually deified they did possess a kind of ·divine right to rule' and a unique position between God and man. Later, under Islam, rulers took the appellation 'the shadow of God upon earth' and similar titles. The institution of kingship has long and deep roots in Iranian history, but a survey of that history reveals varying facets of rule in Iran.

The Iranians, who gave their name and tongue to the country, were originally nomads from Central Asia closely related to the Indians who conquered India. We can only surmise that the Indo-Iranians left their Indo-European home-land to wander southwards probably sometime in the second millennium BC. They obviously did not come all at once in one invasion but spread over the Iranian plateau in different waves or migrations. We are not concerned with the history of these early migrating Iranians, but what is important at the present day is to realize that this nomadic background has had echoes in Iranian literature and mores down to the present. Just as the city Arab today regards the bedouin of the desert with a kind of nostalgia, believing that the nomad is the 'true Arab' who speaks a purer Arabic than in the towns and who maintains the old Arab bedouin traditions, so the Persian also has a perhaps sublimated longing for the golden age of knights on horseback and their valour. A high regard for the nomad is, of course, almost lacking in the modern settled Persian since the nomads are usually Turks, Arabs, Baluchis or Lurs rather than 'true Persians'. Also the settled folk have suffered too much in the past from the depredations of the nomads to have cause for anything but hate. The conflict between the steppe and the sown is age-old in Iran. Nonetheless, down to the Islamization of Iran, in the tenth and eleventh centuries, the memory, albeit faint and oft transformed, of the 'nomadic' past was still alive among the people.

We learn about Indo-Iranian or Aryan society primarily from the Indian hymns to the gods, the Vedas, and we may assume that the original Iranians had similar beliefs and organization. For all nomads living in the steppes or deserts life is difficult and to survive society must be organized along military lines. A tribe on the move must have been very similar to an ancient army, if not even better disciplined. This was one reason why the nomads were always more superior militarily to settled folk. Eastern Iran was probably sparsely inhabited by aborigines, the vestiges of whom at the present day may be the Brahuis, Dravidian speakers of Baluchistan, and the Burushaskis of Hunza. In any case, the Iranians were able to maintain their old Indo-European traditions and beliefs better in eastern Iran than in western Iran. The history of eastern Iran is the tale of Indian-Iranian conflicts and contacts, with relatively little known about the aborigines.

When the Iranians came into western Iran in the ninth and eighth centuries BC they found ancient cultures and different settled peoples with traditions of their own. Scholars who study ancient Iran frequently neglect the important background of the Urartians in Armenia and Azerbaijan, the

Manneans in present Kurdistan, the Elamites in the south and others. These peoples had founded cities and carried on trade for centuries with the lowlands of Mesopotamia and were engaged in struggles against the expanding power of Assyria. The Medes, the Persians, and other Iranian tribes were new-comers on the scene of Near Eastern history, although they may well have found traces of previous Indo-European bands which had wandered into the Near East and had been then absorbed by the indigenous population. So the Iranians who settled in western Iran, primarily the Medes and the Persians, became the heirs of ancient Mesopotamia, while the Iranians of the east better maintained their ancient traditions. This fundamental difference between eastern and western Iran, in my opinion, helps to explain differences which exist down to the present.

In eastern Iran the old society with clear divisions of family, clan and tribe persisted much longer than in the west. The tribal divisions became the basis of the Achaemenid satrapies in eastern Iran, while the backbone of society was the clan, which after the family was the most important unit of loyalty. In western Iran, however, the clan lost its importance after the Medes and Persians settled among their subjects. The family, or even extended family, usurped the position of the clan, while the nation took over the role of the tribe. This development is revealed in the cuneiform inscriptions of Darius and Xerxes where the royal family of the Achaemenids displaces the clan of the Pasargadai in importance and the *dahyu*—'country', 'nation'—becomes more potent than the tribe in men's loyalties. A new imperial Iranian tradition was born from the marriage of traditional Aryan society and the ancient Near East, and this was the world empire of the Achaemenids.

The one world of the Achaemenids was a tolerant one compared to the previous states of the Egyptians, Babylonians and Assyrians. We know of Cyrus' policy towards the Jews in Mesopotamia whom he allowed to return to Palestine from their Babylonian captivity. Darius fostered law codes for the Babylonians, Egyptians and other subjects, while religious tolerance was especially marked in comparison with the past. Although the Persians ruled most of the Near East in a comparatively benevolent fashion, there was no doubt that the Persians and their kinsmen the Medes were the rulers in perhaps the earliest dual monarchy or empire in recorded history.

Western ideas about the early Persians are derived, of course, from their enemies the Greeks. Yet even with the enmity, we find in our sources an admiration for the people who had conquered so many nations and who taught their children how to ride a horse, shoot a bow, and speak the truth. The 'king' to the Greeks always meant the Persian king of kings, a title which had been borne by the rulers of the Urartians in earlier times but which really came into prominence only under the Achaemenids. This imperial tradition has survived in Persian history down to the present.

The Achaemenid monarch ruled over Iranians and non-Iranians, which was the great dichotomy of the empire. Thus was the element of exclusiveness in rule for the Persians now joined to the greater concept of the ecumenical state with many peoples, many customs and many religions. Unlike past empires where, for example, the god of Assur had conquered the gods of other cities and states, the Achaemenids supported the doctrine of separateness in various kingdoms but under the universal ruler the Achaemenid king of kings.

Under the Achaemenids an elaborate court protocol developed which continued throughout history. Herodotus tells us of the Achaemenids' love of titles and honorifics, while Theophylactus Simocatta, a Byzantine historian, repeats the same observation about the Sasanians, and we know that the Qajar rulers of the nineteenth century revelled in titles, honorifics or special names, such that they even replaced personal names. For example, the large Farmanfarmaian family today has its name from the title of a Qajar prince, not his family or personal name. The titulary of Persians has been an outstanding trait of theirs through the centuries. This concern with proper forms and language can be observed in what little we know of the Achaemenid court, among the Sasanians, and in the everyday flowery speech of the recent past. The polite usages of the Persian language are frequently puzzling to foreigners trying to learn the language, especially those foreigners who have lost the grace of formalities in their own society.

It is interesting that the mores of the imperial Achaemenid court influenced the subject kingdoms, the provincial or satrapal courts which were but smaller copies of the splendour of the central government. After the fall of the Achaemenid empire by the conquests of Alexander the Great *circa* 330 BC the imperial Achaemenid tradition continued to flourish in provincial centres. Under the Diadochi and especially the Seleucids there existed a double bureaucracy and a double culture in Iran, the old Achaemenid and the new Greek. The former, however, was not just Iranian but cosmopolitan; for example, Aramaic was the *lingua franca* of the Achaemenid empire rather than Old Persian, written in cuneiform characters and only known from inscriptions. In the course of Seleucid rule Greeks and Persians borrowed much from each other and Iran was certainly greatly influenced by the culture of the Hellenic conquerors. Although much has been written about the meeting between the Greek *polis* and the Iranian *imperium*, when one considers the subsequent history of Iran the effects of Hellenic civilization on the mass of the Persian people are seen to have been few and decidedly secondary in importance.

One seemingly new concept of rule appears in Hellenistic times in Iran, and indeed everywhere as a sign of the times. That is a new belief in the divinity of kings, not in the old sense of the king as a son of the gods, but in a new messianic role. The later Seleucids used titles on their coins such as *epiphanes* 'manifest', *soter* 'saviour', and the like. This may be the period when soteriological beliefs became prominent in Zoroastrianism, the dominant religion of the ancient Iranians. It would seem that belief in saviours arose in the Hellenistic period everywhere as an answer to a kind of bankruptcy both in institutionalized religions and in rational and philosophical thought best exemplified by the Greeks. Whatever and whenever its origins, we may postulate a new importance for the messianic nature of kingship in ancient Iran at this time.

The idea of a saviour, however, is not that of an earthly king who stands above men and leads them, but one who knows suffering and can understand the sorrows of common men. So in Iran this aspect is present in what one might call the myth of the founder of a dynasty, which myth has become almost a dogma in the Persian concept of kingship. The general features of this myth, which becomes then real history for the Persians, are relationship to the preceding dynasty or possessing royal blood, persecution with flight or exile, and concealment of royal origins, plus a difficult life among nomads or peasants. Finally a son, grandson, or later descendant of the exile by manifest signs and qualities receives recognition and the *khvarnah* or imperial glory descends upon him so that he founds a new dynasty.

Of course many widespread common features and variations are found in this Iranian myth, and we may call to mind certain parallels as the story of Moses in the bullrushes, the childhood of the Assyrian king Sargon II, perhaps Romulus and Remus and many others. We are not interested here in the origins of such tales, or even whether they were true or not. What is important in our context is that they were believed to be true by Persians throughout their history. It is part of their lore of kingship and rule and so it is important for our understanding of the people of Iran.

The story of the rise of Cyrus, as reported by Ctesias, Xenophon, Herodotus and others, has all of the required facets of the history of the founder of a new dynasty, in his case of the Achaemenids. Justin tells us that Arsaces, the founder of the Parthian dynasty, was a Bactrian noble serving under the Greek kings of eastern Iran, who was forced to flee and go into exile after which fortune smiled on him. Sasan, the eponymous ancestor of the Sasanians was a descendant of the Achaemenid kings who lived in secret with Kurdish shepherds before he was recognized and elevated. Ismail, founder of the Safavid dynasty, also lived in exile and privation before he became shah. And the founder of the present dynasty, Reza Shah Pahlavi, was a poor army officer, who according to many tales had royal blood in his veins, some even saying he was a true descendant of the Sasanians or the Safavids. This brings us to another point, the question of legitimacy in Persian kingship, itself a strong tradition.

Cyrus, and the Achaemenids, established the first human symbol of legitimacy for the Persians. Cyrus was not only the great conqueror and benevolent ruler but also the sum of all virtues for the Persians. He was the father of his people, and his successors ruled because they were descended from that idealized person. Even long after the fall of the Achaemenid empire local rulers justified their limited rule by claiming descent from the Achaemenids. Perhaps the best known monarchs who did this were Mithradates of Pontus, strong opponent of the Romans who was defeated by Pompey, and Antiochus of Commagene who erected large statues to his ancestors on Nimrud Dagh, a mountain in present southwest Turkey. The latter also, however, claimed descent from Alexander the Great. When the Greeks conquered the Near East they introduced a new figure of legitimacy, Alexander the Great, and he competed with the Achaemenids for the crown of legitimacy. In this contest, although Alexander was successful in many parts of the Near East, he was not successful in Iran. Some dynasties, like that of Commagene, exalted both Greeks and Persians as their ancestors in the syncretism so characteristic of the Hellenistic age, but in Iran Alexander did not replace the Achaemenids.

The Achaemenid principle of legitimacy was replaced in

Iran by the advent of a new dynasty and a new hero, the founder of the Sasanian empire, Ardashir Papakan, about the year 226 after Christ. Sasanian legitimacy survived long into Islamic times with many local Iranian princes claiming descent from the dynasty overthrown by the Arabs. Nonetheless, the pattern was changed by the Islamization of Iran, a process which spread over several centuries of Muslim rule. Under Islam a new and a more potent hero appeared on the scene, 'Ali, closely related to the family of the prophet Muhammad.

The Persians accepted the cause of the house of the prophet with alacrity, for it coincided with their traditions of legitimacy. Since the family of Muhammad descended through his son-in-law 'Ali, the latter's cause became the cause of the Persians who even, in tradition, joined one of 'Ali's sons in marriage with a daughter of Yazdegird, the last Sasanian king. It is well known that Khurasan, or eastern Iran, played a leading role in the overthrow of the Umayyad Caliphate in 750 and the establishment of the new 'Abbasid Caliphate. The new Caliphate followed Iranian traditions in the eyes of many. The reasons for this revolution were many and complicated, but we are concerned here only with the concept of legitimacy and kingship in Iran, and the new religion of Islam added an important new element to the old traditions of rule in Iran.

The old traditions were not replaced or abandoned; they had to be reconciled with the new realities. As a matter of fact the ancient traditions were assembled and recorded in the tenth century when Islam had already won over the Persians. They were preserved for us primarily in the Persian National Epic, the *Shahname* or 'book of kings' by Firdosi, written of course in poetry. In it the old east Iranian cycle of stories about local kings and Zoroaster had been joined to the west Iranian historical or secular tales of Cyrus, Ardashir and others, with the semi-nomadic, chivalric, or even feudal stories of the mythical east Iranian heroes such as Rustam and Isfandiyar clearly more beloved by Iranians than the more prosaic tales of western Iran. In the *Shahname* the story of the revolt of Kaveh the blacksmith, and other stories as well, show the concern of Persians with the idea of the legitimate king and the right to revolt against an illegitimate ruler. Fortunately for Muslim Persians, the Arabs were not concerned with pre-Islamic history, since for them history really began with the prophet. So the Persian Muslims could retain and exalt their past and even consider it the logical background for the new life under Islam. At the same time that past was idealized and lost most of its historical reality. Then a new impetus was given to the ancient traditions of rule by new conquerors from the steppes of Central Asia.

The Turkish invasion or rather inundation of the Near East profoundly altered the face of the entire area. From the time of the Seljuk conquests of the eleventh century down to World War I the rulers of the Near East were predominantly Turkish in origin, for here again, a new legitimacy was created by the new people. All of Anatolia, Azerbaijan, and other areas partially, were Turkified in the course of time, and the present division of the three main peoples of the Near East, Turks, Persians and Arabs was formed. It came almost to be a folk belief that Turks were destined to rule, as the Persians were masters of the arts, while the Arabs concerned themselves with religion, a parallel to the medieval European tradition that the Germans held the *imperium,* the French *magisterium,* while the Italians were concerned with *sacerdotium.* Again what people believed frequently overshadowed what really was.

The new heroic, even super-human, figure, the founder of a new dynasty, was not a Turk but a Mongol, Chinggis Khan. The Mongols ruled Iran for over a century, and like the Golden Horde in Russia they strongly influenced the people of the country. We cannot discuss Far Eastern influences, such as art, which entered Iran in the wake of the Mongol conquests, but Central Asiatic, nomadic principles of rule, first brought by the Turks, were now greatly strengthened by the Mongol rulers. The para-military state bureaucracy established in Iran by them continued to flourish, one might say, down to the Qajar dynasty, and is evidenced by the Turkish and even Mongolian titles such as Il-khan, Topchi-bashi, and *darugha* used in Iran in Safavid times. After Chinggis came a Turk Timur, or Tamerlane, who continued the Mongol tradition. His descendants in eastern Iran and Central Asia later contributed to a cultural flowering called the Timurid age. One of the Timurids, Babur, invaded India and started the Moghul dynasty of India where Persian was the language of the court and of learned intercourse.

The religious part of the right to rule had declined, especially after the end of the 'Abbasid Caliphate at the hands of the Mongols in 1258. Furthermore the Turks were Sunnis for the most part, and the Shiites in Iran, who were not inconsiderable in numbers, were excluded from the rule. Their day came, however, at the end of the fifteenth century when a most fortunate combination of dynastic and religious legitimacy enabled the both secular and religious leader Shaikh Ismail to establish the Safavid dynasty. Shaikh Haidar the father of Ismail, claimed legitimacy both as heir of the Timurids through the dominant Turkomen dynasties then ruling western Iran and in descent from the prophet Muhammad himself. Thus modern Iran was founded on the principle of the union of church and state in the personage of the shah. In a certain sense the Islamic conception of the Caliph was revived again in the Safavid ruler. Of course the religious side of rule again later declined because there was no real church in Islam, and among the Shiites the learned doctors of law and religion were the real leaders of the faith rather than the ruler.

The splendour of the Safavid court set the tone in form and protocol for the later Qajars and for the present. The modern history of Iran can be dated from the beginning of Safavid rule and Shah 'Abbas who embellished Isfahan with its superb architectural monuments, became the new hero for the future. Most ruined mosques, or other Islamic buildings in Iran, the dates of which are unknown, are usually ascribed to Shah 'Abbas by the local people.

The Safavid state brought new factors to the old concepts of Iranian kingship, for it was necessary to have a new solidarity complex since Turks, many of whom could not even speak Persian, were ruling everywhere. The achievement of the Safavids was the creation of a 'national' state comprising all of Iran, the counterpart in Islamic times of the old Sasanian state. Just as the Zoroastrian church provided the theoretical and spiritual basis for the latter, so the basis for the national sentiment of Safavid Iran was Shiism. In the new state neither language nor race provided the bond of unity but it was religion. Henceforth 'Persian' meant Shiite even though the Persian spoke Turkish or another language.

The Safavid shah was also head of the primarily Turkish tribal military-religious brotherhoods, the members of which were called by outsiders Qizilbash, and as such, he was accorded almost divine honours. In time, however, the religious leadership of the shah atrophied and the secular side of his rule became dominant. Later when the Safavid rulers broke the power of the Qizilbash chiefs the theocratic basis of the shah's rule was also shattered. The transformation of the Qizilbash fiefs into crown lands and the creation of an army loyal to and dependent on the shah did not provide for a new principle of rule to replace the religious nationalism of the Qizilbash brotherhood. But the authoritativeness and the prestige of the office and person of the shah did continue to exist and later the Qajars inherited it.

One might characterize the more than a century of Qajar rule as a kind of moribund kingdom living on the past Safavid traditions. The Qajars were a Turkish tribe but the state became less one in which Turks ruled with their army while Persians governed with the bureaucracy, and more a state where Persian language and culture, and of course adherence to the Shiite faith, became the requisites of holding power and authority. There was no new theory of state or of rule but

c

only a continuation of past traditions with little novelty to fit the changing times. The impact of the West shattered the old order of things in Iran as elsewhere in the Orient at the turn of the twentieth century.

The first great change came before the Persians were prepared for it, and the result of the creation of a constitution in 1906, and the formation of a parliament shortly thereafter, was chaos. Many Persians could not understand what relation the constitution and the *majlis* had to the ruling shah, for was not the ruler still the 'shadow of God upon earth'? Before the manifold problems of the new order could be even studied World War I occurred, then more chaos, and finally disintegrating Iran was rescued by a strong man Reza Shah Pahlavi

Reza Shah decided that Iran was not ready for the paraphernalia of Western parliamentary government so he ruled benevolently by fiat. Yet he passionately believed in a modern, powerful Iran which could prosper, in his opinion, only if the underbrush of the Safavid and Qajar past could be cleared away. This meant the divorce of church and state, the creation of a new secular society. The religious leaders became the symbols of the old and hence 'reactionary' order of life. So in the period between the World Wars the new Iran was fashioned on Western models. But Iran could not take over the ideologies, the traditions, or even the symbols of rule of France or England. Like his neighbour Kemal Ataturk in Turkey Reza Shah looked to the pre-Islamic past of Iran to provide the spiritual and emotional groundwork on which to build the Westernized state. There was a great revival of interest in Firdosi's *Shahname* and in the lore and lessons of the ancient past, glorified into a golden age. It was as though Iran had slumbered for a millennium and a half under the baneful rule of Arab Islam, and was now to be revived with a new Iranian nationalism bereft of the stultifying influence of Islam. Needless to say, many Persians including, of course, the religious leaders thought such sentiments were not only blasphemous but stupid. Nonetheless, the position of the Shahinshah was now that of leader of a huge enterprise, the modernization of Iran, as well as commander-in-chief of the army and supreme judge. No longer was the shah to be 'defender of the faith', or 'shadow of God upon earth', and it was even questionable whether he would remain possessor of the spiritual charisma of the king of kings. The age of Mohammed Reza Pahlavi is one in which the parliament, the court, and the religious leaders, the *'ulama,* are all uncertain not only as to who determines what, or who rules whom, but also what the future *'asabiyya,* the future principle of rule, the future charisma will be. One cannot ignore the past, pre-Islamic as well as Islamic, and Iran will have to integrate that past into the ever shrinking One World of the future. With her manifold traditions and her genius for integration, Iran should be able to forge a new *'asabiyya* which will include the best of the past and something of the future, and should enable Iran to survive the shocks of an atomic age.

CHAPTER III

Cultural Syncretism

IT has been said that three factors serve as the roots of a culture; its rationality or pursuit of thought, its religion or the relation of its persons to the universe, and its appreciation of art and beauty. Society then binds them together to make in this case an Iranian culture. What has been the Persian ideal of art and beauty throughout the centuries?

At once one may point out a special feature of the Iranian aesthetic taste in all periods of history, which is, on the whole, the predominance of decoration over representation. This is especially true, in my opinion, of Achaemenid and Sasanian art while Parthian and the early Islamic art of Iran are both perhaps better described as expressionist rather than merely decorative. By this is meant that the underlying idea of spirit is paramount in the art rather than appearance or what is seen. As is well known, the Persians have been ever the artists of the Near East, and world music, painting and architecture all have been enriched by Persian contributions.

Achaemenid art, mainly preserved in architectural ruins, was explicit and straightforward with a minimum of involved symbolism and spiritual meaning. It was an imperial art showing the glory of the world state, and as such it was syncretistic or even international. This is not the place to discuss questions of the influence of Greek art upon Persian art or vice versa. Suffice it to say that while we find Greek, Assyrian and even Egyptian elements in Iranian art, the last was distinctive by being a synthesis or summation of the already ancient past of the Near East. The Assyrian bas-reliefs from Khorsabad and elsewhere, many of which may be seen in the British Museum, tell stories of the hunts of the Assyrian kings, their conquests of cities and the captives they took after a victory. The Achaemenid bas-reliefs, on the contrary, tell no story but only portray, in a conventionalized manner, the idealized court of the king of kings. The tribute bearers at Persepolis do not bring their gifts as conquered peoples or captives, but as subjects of the great king of kings should do in the nature of things, in a well-ordered empire and universe. It is as though the Achaemenids were proclaiming to the world that a world state ruled by the Persians was indeed a paradise on earth, not the heavenly paradise of later usage but more in the original meaning of the Iranian word, the king's enclosed park. There does not seem to be much spirituality in Achaemenid art, comparable to Buddist art or even later Iranian art, but we must not forget that much has not survived.

The invasion of Alexander the Great put an end to the Achaemenid court art, even though it probably survived for a while in provincial centres. The art of the Hellenistic age was not only syncretistic but also, like the religious and philosophical *Zeitgeist,* abstract and expressionist. In Iran the prosaic age of the Achaemenids turned into the epic and chivalric age of the Parthians, and inner meaning was emphasized over external appearance. Unfortunately little has been found in Persia proper from Parthian times, but on the fringes of Iran, from the desert city of Hatra in Mesopotamia and from Begram in present Afghanistan we obtain in the arts glimpses of concern with individual suffering and with mystical serenity. Certainly the sculptured heads found at both sites seem more realistic than previous sculptures, but they do not represent individuals, rather they show, for example, the deformed individual in general, the sufferer in general. Again, they tell no story but portray states or feelings, most of them unhappy.

The architecture of the Achaemenids seems to have been

inspired primarily from Greek prototypes, though the overly tall columns, the bull capitals, and other features are Persian in inspiration. New forms of architecture come from Iran in the post-Achaemenid period, the most notorious of which are the liwan and the squinch. The dominant characteristic of Parthian sculptures or bas-reliefs is frontality, which gives an impression of unreality in keeping with the times.

At the same time nomadic, Central Asian influences are found in the polychromy and the gold incrustation of small objects. This style was carried by the Sarmatians into Europe where the Goths learned it and finally, after adaptations, it influenced Merovingian art. This raises the matter of nomadic cultural influences on Iran.

We have said that the conflicts between steppe and sown, Turk and Iranian, and many other seeming dualisms, were significant in the history of Iran. When Iran was strong and united her influence extended far beyond her borders, especially into Central Asia. This is noticeable under the Achaemenids, Sasanians, and Safavids. The roles were reversed, however, under the Parthians, Seljuks and Mongols. Even before the Achaemenids, the plethora of famous Luristan bronzes, now found in most museums of the world, show Scythian, nomadic influences not only in style, but also in their very purposes, as mouth bits, harness trappings, and other horse decorations. The so-called 'animal style', in its widest application, is the art style of the steppe lands extending from Hungary to the wall of China from pre-historic times down to the Mongols. It influenced Iran and was influenced by Iranian tastes, especially in periods when Iran was flourishing or even actively colonizing the oasis towns of central Asia.

Frequently the visitor to Iran is startled to find contemporary objects made by the Lurs, Kurds or other tribesmen just like objects of three thousand years ago. Such is the tenacity of artistic and cultural traditions in Iran.

Under the Sasanians art became even more decorative. Building on Parthian developments, the Sasanians lost some of the spirit which engendered such art in favour of pure decoration or symbolism. Yet the new symbolism did not conceal any hidden meaning, rather it was in a sense representative of the feudal, symbol-conscious society. A tree of life which had a religious significance in previous centuries was now stylized and became the coat-of-arms of a feudal family. Furthermore art became ever more stylized and involved. The media too had changed, for example, from earlier stone to clay and stucco. Greater possibilities for expression obtained in more plastic material which offered less resistance and challenge to the artist. Such was the somewhat over-formalized, even decadent, Sasanian art when the Arabs conquered Iran.

The Islamic interdiction on representation of the human body in any form is well known. The sophisticated Persians who became Muslims could not believe that this ban applied to them who would not mistake a representation for the actuality. The Persians were not idol worshippers as were some benighted grasshopper-eating Arab tribes, against whom the prophet had preached. Consequently, whereas in Semitic lands, where the Arabs dominated, eventually portraits vanished from the artistic scene, in Iran we have paintings of human figures from all periods of her Islamic history. Likewise the drinking of wine, condemned in Islam, was never banished from Iranian tables, although periods of prohibition are not unknown in Iran's history. Reasons for this undoubtedly could be found, but one may remark that generally the Persians, though as devout as any others, basically did not consider such matters as part of one's religion, or at least not central to it.

Later Islamic art is overwhelmingly Persian art. This is not to deny originality to the glassmakers, the bookbinders and the architects of Syria, Egypt and elsewhere, but in the principal fine arts, painting and music, the Persians rank supreme in the Islamic world. It is generally accepted that Sasanian music is the foundation of the traditional music of the Near East at present, or before the West entered the scene. We know about Sasanian music from a number of sources, and the great influence on the Armenians, Arabs and other peoples of the Near East seems certain. This is not the place to go into technical details regarding that music, instruments, or other matters. The place of the village minstrel, a pre-Islamic Iranian institution, in the dissemination of the lays of ancient Iran among the populace, and in general as a teacher and edifier of the folk, is still important. Every tea house had a bard or musician in the old days, but now they have radios over which occasionally traditional songs may still be heard.

The glorious age of Persian miniature painting is the late Timurid and early Safavid periods. In this era, as at no other time or place in the Near East, we know of the individual artists, masters similar to the Renaissance painters in individuality if not in style. The greatest Persian miniaturist was Behzad who lived in Herat at the end of the fifteenth century. His exquisite details are unmatched and his miniature paintings when offered sell for high prices. The refined Safavid age produced the splendid carpets and the superb tile work on such architectural masterpieces as the mosque of the shah and the mosque of Shaikh Lutfullah on the great square, formerly used as a polo field, in Isfahan. When people speak of Persian art they usually think of Safavid art.

During the Qajar dynasty European influences became ever stronger and a baroque followed by a 'Victorian' period have condemned Qajar art to the basement or attic. Some Qajar painting, inlaid work, and woodcarving, however, represent a *tour de force* in attention to minute detail and intricacy. Perhaps one might characterize this art as one in which the craft dominates aesthetics. In craftsmanship the Persians are still excellent and hand work is highly prized, not only by foreigners but by local collectors.

Before mentioning the artistic revival under Reza Shah and the present, it may be well to consider a social aspect implied in the patronage of the fine arts, a wide subject which can only be briefly touched upon here. In Europe in the late Middle

Ages and in the Renaissance the arts flourished in part because of the many patrons, the princes in minor courts or members of noble families, by whom artists were richly rewarded. To a certain extent the same applied to Iran, for the feudal families were always important. In Achaemenid times we hear of the six helpers of Darius when he obtained the throne and the special privileges their families held at court. Later the great feudal families of the Suren, Karen, and others maintained their own armies and their own courts, and, of course, the geography of Iran was admirably suited for independent provincial lords. Late into Islamic times many families traced their descent from Sasanian feudal families and the aristocracy of Iran has survived to the present in families of former Qajar princes.

To return, after this brief digression, to the arts, we come to the modern revival under Reza Shah. By World War I the traditional arts and crafts of Iran had fallen on evil days since they were unable to compete with cheap European mass-produced textiles, dyes, and various wares. Reza Shah sought to revive the traditional arts by organizing a school in Tehran and institutionalizing the crafts. There is no question but that he saved some of the crafts which were on the verge of dying out. On the other hand, the state patronage of the arts some-times failed to produce originality or a fresh, new spirit. The buildings erected by the shah in neo-Achaemenid or neo-Sasanian styles were invariably deplorable from the aesthetic point of view. But these were early attempts to find a new path combining the ancient traditions of Iran with modern exigencies. Not until the artists, and indeed those in other fields, such as literature and language, gave up their attempts to ignore the millennium and a half of Islamic culture in Iran, did reason return to the intellectual development of modern Iran. The new styles of architecture utilizing tiles, such as the tomb of Sa'di near Shiraz and several new bank buildings, while subject perhaps to some criticism, are, nonetheless, so much more in harmony with the Iranian spirit than the neo-

Achaemenid buildings that one can only applaud the present and hopefully future direction of the fine arts in Iran.

There is another social feature of the arts in Iran which is worthy of note. The peoples of neighbouring countries generally speaking have shown little interest in the antiquities and historic arts of their own lands. But in Iran there is a long legacy of interest in collecting antiques and even specialized hobbies such as old glass, coins, miniatures, wood work, manuscripts, and the like. Tehran today has many collectors and specialists who are interested in local objects even more than are collectors of Iranian art in Paris, London or New York. This is one indication of the place the arts holds in the hearts of the people. Persian antiques, as well as forgeries, frequently sell for more to individual Persian collectors than to dealers or museums in America or Europe. This again shows that the Persian, although he may accept foreign influences, still is proud to hold on to his own native culture which has a powerful attraction for the inhabitants of that land.

Finally another sophistication of the Persians should be noted, the art of forgery. Since the Communist conquest of China, Persia probably now holds the palm for excellence in forgeries. In the old Colonial days in India British army officers provided a profitable market for the expert forgers of Rawalpindi, but the art of forgery is not to be mistaken for a purely mercenary enterprise. Forgery in Iran was and is an art or craft to be enjoyed in and for itself. Furthermore forgeries were not made just to secure money from unknowing foreigners. Just as some modern painters forged Renaissance works of art to show that they could equal the masters, so Persian forgers were not loathe to fool their own countrymen, but the best was to fool an expert, be he Persian or foreigner. That is why many still find it difficult to understand why the Persian forger goes to almost incredible pains to produce a work hardly able to repay him for the effort lavished on the forgery.

While the subject of forgeries frequently can be painful to

many collectors, it is a game in Iran for most concerned with it. It is probably well described as an extension of bazaar psychology, known to most foreigners who have made purchases in traditional Oriental bazaars. Sometimes the novice, for example a strong-willed American matron, can obtain bargains which the experienced native cannot match simply because the merchant wishes to be rid of a customer who does not observe protocol and the niceties of bazaar procedure, wherein the matching of wits is just as important as the end sale. The Persian is full of subtleties and his code of respect and formalities, called *tashrifat,* is both difficult to translate and to understand.

The *tashrifat* of the Persians is probably the most apparent or distinguishing characteristic of the people. It is especially revealed in the language. For example, instead of saying simply 'he has come' *amad,* one could use a figure of speech such as *tashrif farma shudand,* literally 'his honour has made command', but hardly translatable. In the old days before Westernization, many formalities, similar to the tea ceremony of Japan, were observed with strictness, for they were the essence of life in Iranian society. The flavour of some of this can be gained from the novels of James Morier, especially his *Hajji Baba of Isfahan,* incidentally almost as much a classic in Persian translation as in the English original.

We have returned to the subject of the ambivalent Persian temperament, and to *taqiyeh* or *kitman,* well epitomized in Sa'di's writings which have served as textbooks for Persian children learning to read for many generations. Right at the start of his book the *Gulistan* or 'rose garden' the moral is expressed that a white lie which brings goodwill is better than the truth which causes trouble. At least here the Persians express openly what others may believe yet conceal.

CHAPTER IV

The Flowering of Literature

THE pursuit of thought leads a Persian to the conclusion that man is not all rational: on the contrary he is predominantly emotional. Persian philosophy, in the popular sense, is expressed in poetry and in story, and this, it has been said, is where the genius of the people lies. The continuity of Iranian literature and language over two and a half millennia is striking and should be examined.

The earliest profane 'literature' of the Persians is a poor source for generalization since it is found only in the Old Persian cuneiform inscriptions of the Achaemenid kings, principally Darius and his son Xerxes. The tone of the inscriptions of Darius, however, is interesting. For example, in his great inscription at Behistun Darius time and again emphasizes his truthfulness, admonishing the reader to believe what he has written and not consider it a lie. The rebels against him were followers of the Lie, while he Darius followed the Truth. This emphasis on rectitude has caused many scholars to suspect that Darius protests too much and that the king of kings is reflecting the age old concern of Persians with lying. In my opinion inscriptions are special public documents to be believed unless there is a compelling reason why a falsehood should be recorded on stone; but that is not our concern here. Rather we wish to see the thought and aspirations of the Persians as reflected in their writings throughout history. Much of Persian literature is concerned with religion or influenced by it, so the religious attitudes of the Persians are fundamental to an understanding of his literature. We will discuss those attitudes in the next chapter, while in this one we shall be concerned with genres of literature, changes in the vehicle of expression and social implications of literary output.

Perhaps a fruitful consideration of the Old Persian inscriptions would be to compare them with similar inscriptions in more recent times. Unfortunately we do not know of any of the latter except one royal inscription beside the bas-relief of Fath 'Ali Shah the second Qajar ruler at the site of Bibi Shahrbanu near Tehran. Unfortunately it is illegible. One may, however, surmise the tenor of that inscription from other contemporary sources, so that a hypothetical comparison between the declarations of Darius and Fath 'Ali Shah could be made. The former is straightforward, proud but not arrogant, and exhibits confidence and a certain dignity. The inscription of Fath 'Ali Shah might have been characterized by excessive hyperbole, filled with illusions, and not saying much of anything since the reader would not believe it anyway, so that form rather than content would prevail.

The Avesta, a piece of literature, is in great measure too difficult to understand to draw any conclusions from it. Furthermore, it is in a special class of sacred hymnology comparable to the Vedas of India or the Book of Psalms and considerations of metre or cadence as well as content are beyond our interests here.

The literature of the Parthian period had a great influence in later times and down to the present. For the minstrels or troubadours called *gosan* kept the romantic lays of eastern Iran alive and this oral literature is what we have left of pre-Islamic secular literature. On reading the *Shahname* of Firdosi one can sense the transition from an old world to a new, and one wonders how much of the tone of the poem springs from the circumstances of life proper to Firdosi's own day. The danger of claiming a great about face in the history of the Iranians should be avoided since we do have continuity, and the seemingly great divisions in the history of the land may be really merely the reflection of a special emphasis on a mood or on mores which were always present, possibly dormant, but not previously emphasized. This has led some scholars to claim a great break or crisis in Iranian thought between pre-Islamic realism *cum* optimism and post-Islamic mysticism and pessimism. I, for one, do not believe that the well-known interest in mysticism found in later Persian poetry was totally absent in pre-Islamic times.

The impact of Islam, on the other hand, cannot be minimized, for the change in poetry, for example, is there for all to see. Sasanian poetry in the Pahlavi language was poor in comparison to the tremendous flowering of New Persian poetry later, and we may go further to assert that the ancient poetry was based on a syllabic principle without consideration of the quantity of the vowels. This was later harmonized with the quantitative prosody of the Arabs, itself probably derived from the Greeks, to form the wonderful poetry of the New Persian. Rhyme, of course, was always significant. It was Arabic, the international language or the Latin of the Near East, which gave Persian the richness and flexibility to become a world literature. Think of the poverty of Anglo-Saxon without the Norman French or Latin influence!

The flowering of New Persian literature in the tenth and eleventh centuries signified more than the Islamization of Iran; it meant that Islam as a culture had become international and not simply tied to the Arabic language and the mores of the desert bedouin. In a very real sense the Persians made of Islam a truly ecumenical civilization, and in so doing, they were repeating what their Achaemenid ancestors had done for the ancient Near East.

The new Persian literature reflected the golden age of Islamic thought, religious and philosophical, but, of course, primarily in poetry, where the new techniques were derived in great part from the Arabs. Immediately the names of Omar Khayyam, Jalal al-Din Rumi, Hafez, and others, come to mind and the dominant motif of all, save perhaps Omar, can be expressed in the word mysticism. Mystical verse is regarded by most Persian literati as their chief contribution to world literature, and certainly this is the genre in which the great poets of Iran have excelled. The result of preoccupation with mystical themes brought special meanings to ordinary words; for example, ordinary expressions of love could have their usual meanings as well as special senses of union with God, while imagery of wine drinking could also denote stages on the path of the mystic in his search for ultimate reality. There is a kind of melancholy strand in classical New Persian literature, a kind of pessimism which ends in resignation and takes refuge in Allah, who alone knows best. But this does not monopolize Persian literature, since there is a great variety of outlooks on life, a testimony to the manysidedness of Persian individualism. Soviet scholars of Persian literature, however, have found entirely different criteria for an interpretation of the literary history of Iran.

For many Soviet scholars Persian literature can be divided into two tendencies, the democratic-folk and the feudal-aristocratic. For them the periodization of Persian literature falls together with the development of social stages in the political and social history of Iran, and the literature is a reflection of social conflicts in history. The different sides of the conflicts can be termed progressive or reactionary. The history of New Persian literature for Marxists can be divided into three periods, from the ninth to the fifteenth century, from the sixteenth to the nineteenth, and the modern age. In the first period literature was, in its best representatives, related to the common people, their hopes and fears. Later literature becomes more artificial, didactic and panegyric. Modern literature shows new social consciousness and a realization of many injustices.

Certainly protests against tyranny and social injustice are interesting phenomena not only in Persian literature, but in the history of the land. Mass movements can be traced even in the pre-Islamic history of Iran, and communism, in the original sense of the word, flourished in several periods of Iranian history long before there was a Russia. One of these fascinating epochs was during the Sasanian empire when a religious reformer called Mazdak preached not only a sharing of the wealth, but also of women and children. At the end of the sixth century A.D. the Mazdakites even secured the adherence of the ruler Kavad. The resulting chaos was brought to an end by Chosroes, son of Kavad, surnamed 'of the immortal soul', who bloodily suppressed the Mazdakites and then instituted a series of sweeping reforms in the bureaucracy and the economy of the country. There were, it seems, many writings about Mazdak which have not survived, but he must have made a great impression not only on his contemporaries but also on later generations since his name became synonymous with 'heretic' or rebel against the government. Under Islam we hear of many neo-Mazdakite revolts, especially in eastern Iran.

What is important for the present is to realize that social revolts and demands for justice are old in Iran. The Shiite form of Islam in itself is a protest group by origin, and *mullahs* and *mujtahids,* the religious leaders of the country, have been prominent in denouncing government excesses, and they were the leaders of the Constitutional movement at the turn of the century.

The fatalism of the Oriental is a favourite image of the Westerner, but the fatalism has never prevented protests and uprisings, at least in Iran. Frequently to foreigners a Persian may be like an iceberg; what is seen is small in comparison to what is hidden. Here again we have the different and opposing sides of Persian character, a feature sometimes described as the extremes or the instability of the Persian character by the outsider. At one time the Persian individual may appear completely oblivious to the world, wrapped up in his religious quest for the absolute, or in his art or craft, or in his opium pipe. Later the same Persian can be the most sceptical of people, speaking ironically of everyone and every-

thing and believing in nothing. The human tendency to empha-
size the bad over the good would make of the Persians
the ultimate in hypocrisy, vanity, corruption, ingratitude,
deception, and cowardice. But in the same breath some
Persians can have few peers in recitude, humility, gratefulness,
hospitality and courage. Basically the Persians are a sensitive,
refined and profoundly individualistic people.

Persian literature of the Safavid and even Qajar epochs has
a low standing for many because of the quantity of panegyric
verse produced to glorify a patron and win rewards. It is
sometimes tedious to have to struggle through pages of
hyperbole, frequently with rare words showing the skill
and cleverness of the writer, to reach the meaning of the
exercise. Naturally satire and parody permeate Persian literature, and the verse with double meaning delights the reader.
Much of such writing undoubtedly had a political or other
purpose now difficult to reconstruct, but such writing continues
to evoke high praise if the ridicule and flattery are well done
and properly directed.

The story is told of a poet who wrote an insulting verse
about a ruler in which he said that there was no doubt that
his origin was base (*palid*). He was later captured by the irate
sovereign who asked him why he had written such scurrilous
lines. Since Persian was written cursively and sometimes
without dots, the poet replied that he had really written that
there was no doubt that the ruler's origin was lofty (*buland*),
but a fly had made spots on the paper changing the sense of the
word. The cleverness of that bard was enough to secure his
freedom.

Persian had a great influence in Moghul India and in
Ottoman Turkey, but the literature of Iran by that time had
become artificial since themes and techniques had become
stereotyped and monotonous. The rose and the nightingale
in the writings of a master were superb images, but repeated
a thousand times by lesser poets they became a frozen, un-
interesting subject. Refinement of language in countless ways

became the convention of the mass of literature in more recent times, and the same was true of the Persian poetry and prose written in India or in the Ottoman realm. Both the forms and the spirit of literature, especially poetry, were fixed in the bondage of the past and indeed the past weighed heavily on the Persian.

Modern literature has changed and broken with traditional forms and motifs, and in a real sense it has been in the vanguard of the great social and political changes occurring in Iran in the past half century. The impact of the West and the rising nationalism of the Orient gave an impetus to new kinds of writing. The drama had existed in Iran mainly in the shape of religious plays concerned with the death of Husain son of the Caliph 'Ali, or related subjects. But new plays on the Western model gave a platform for the expression of discontent with the government or the general state of things. The stage became a popular vehicle for radical ideas as well as being a new literary genre. Poetry, of course, is the principal form of literature in the modern age in Persia as in the past. At first the poets maintained the old forms, writing in classical *ghazals* or *qasidas,* but introducing many new subjects, such as the defeat of Russia by Japan in 1905, which made a great impression all over the Orient. New outbursts of patriotism, especially during the Constitutional period, were recorded in poetry but still in traditional metres.

Perhaps the most obvious change in modern literature came during the reign of Reza Shah Pahlavi when a 'purification' of the language was fostered. This meant primarily a replacement of Arabic words by ancient Persian words or even neologisms. This movement, of course, had a profound influence on poets and many of them began to experiment with new forms of poetry as well as new words and new themes. As elsewhere in the Near East, the French were the chief bearers of Western ideas and influences in Iran, and the majority of European foreign words in New Persian are from French. Translations of French novels led to imitation by Persian writers who thus introduced this new genre. With the novel came the use of colloquial speech and even dialects as a literary medium. Perhaps the introduction of the colloquial, spoken language into all forms of literature ended Classicism more than anything else. No doubt the use of colloquial language also helped to increase literacy.

While the modern poetry and prose reflects the more practical everyday concerns of the citizen of Iran, high regard for the traditional Sufi, mystical literature still exists. There have been attacks on the old themes; one writer claimed that the panegyric *qasidas* of court poets contributed to the arrogance and tyranny of shah and nobility, while the Sufi teachings caused pessimism and laziness and the love poetry corrupted the morals.[1] On the whole, however, the old and the new exist side by side, and such is the richness of Persian poetry that there is room for all schools of versification, and probably they will all flourish since an audience can always be found for any and all poetry in Iran.

The existence of a refugee literature in Persian has continued from the late nineteenth century to the present, frequently characterized by bitterness against the government or society of Iran or by profound disillusionment. During the Qajar period refugee writers attacked the despotism of the shahs through emigré newspapers or books. Since the advent of Reza Shah Western Europe and Soviet Russia have provided a haven for anti-government liberals, and since the fall of Dr Mossadegh in 1953, especially the United States, East Germany and other peoples' democracies have experienced an influx of exiles. Persians, wherever they go and however long they remain away from Iran, rarely forget that they are Persians, and in spite of criticism of Iran or even bitterness about the homeland they still are loathe to abandon Persian culture. This is the finest tribute to a land, that in spite of corruption, poverty, or tyranny it exercises such a hold over

[1] Nazim al-Islam Kirmani *Ta'rikh-i Bidari-yi Iraniyan* (History of the Awakening of the Persians) (Tehran, n.d.) 242.

her sons, and Iran does that. The literature of Iran is a great and rich literature with an honoured place in the annals of man, and it is one of the many legacies of the Persians to the world.

CHAPTER V

Dualism in Faith

A RECOGNITION of the forces of good and of evil in the world can be a logical and sensible answer to the many questions raised by a monism. Dualism and dichotomies have always seemed particularly attractive to the mind, and they have also appeared to be optimistic solutions to problems since tripartite divisions and more are frequently too complicated or in other ways unsatisfactory. And Iran is the country of dualism more than any other. We first find it with Zoroaster.

Zoroaster is a fascinating figure in religious history, surely of equal stature with the prophets of the Old Testament. He must have been a great reformer of the ancient Aryan religion common to both Iranians and Indians. The essential features of that old religion, principally as revealed in the Vedas, were sacred hymns of praise to the gods recited at the time of certain sacrifices. Yet the social aspects of this faith were not lacking, for the harmony between gods and men was essential to the functioning of the universe. Zoroaster's message, contained in the Gathas, the oldest part of the Avesta, is ethical in emphasis and sharply distinguishes between good and evil. Man, through the prophet Zoroaster, was brought into a closer relationship, almost a partnership with one deity Ahura Mazda 'the wise Lord', and his life was conditioned by his choice of the good path following Ahura Mazda or of the bad way of Ahriman, the evil spirit. So the religion of Zoroaster came to be known as 'the good religion'.

Later Zoroastrianism followed a characteristically Iranian path of synthesis and compromise, but it always remained a highly moralistic faith and also an optimistic one. Although our information is very scanty, Zoroastrianism hardly escaped the influence of Greek thought, and we may conjecture that differing schools of theology, in the widest significance, developed in Iran. Optimism could not flourish in Iran without the opposite reaction pessimism, and so we find also a belief in inexorable fate, opposing the optimistic dualism which really held to the ultimate triumph of goodness. The belief in fate developed in a movement named after the word for 'fate' or 'time', Zurvanism. It would seem that Zurvanism, in certain periods of the pre-Islamic history of Iran, was the dominant mood of the articulate populace. The word 'mood' is perhaps more appropriate than 'religion' or 'sect', since we have no evidence that there existed a separate church organization of Zurvanism with definite and separate dogmas or rites. Of course other faiths, if not organized 'church religions', probably existed in Iran, not to speak of foreign religions or those of minorities such as the Jews. Unfortunately our sources do little more than mention their existence.

We have already noticed the urge to social justice in pre-Islamic Iran, particularly in the important social-religious movement called Mazdakism which seems to have had affinities with Manichaeism. The need for social and economic reform has always been great in Iran where large feudal land-owners flourished and still flourish. Much land of course could have even a minimum of produce only by extensive irrigation which required some central control. The basis of the wealth and power of the aristocracy has always been land, and the prestige of owning many villages is still important today. Therefore, one might say that a 'feudal' tradition of society and a consequent class structure have been as characteristic of Iranian history as the oasis is of the landscape. The Parthian period of Iran's history is usually cited as the highpoint of 'feudalism', but some form of 'feudalism' seems always to have been present. One should not equate Western European feudalism, however, with what obtained in Iran except in the widest sense.

Persian 'feudalism' has its roots in the extended family, including servants, with the *pater familias,* and this has been the only real unit of loyalty for most Persians down to recent times. In the past, as at the present, it has even taken the place of public responsibility to the detriment of the nation. On the other hand, this family loyalty together with personal ties to others has been a source of strength and stability in Iran. A benevolent landlord was frequently regarded by his peasants as a protector, even from government interferences and exactions. The landlord, usually absentee, was treated as the source of law, order and authority by the villagers under him and this is only now changing albeit slowly.

The point to be emphasized, however, is that in all periods of Iran's past there has been a social content to religion, or put in another way, there have been religious implications of government and society, and not just with the advent of Islam as some scholars have claimed. In the religious sphere the comparison of Manichaeism and Bahaism, I believe, is relevant to our understanding of Iran. Both were violently opposed by the national religions of the time, Zoroastrianism under the Sasanids and Shiite Islam under the Qajars. Both Manichaeism and Bahaism were considered threats to the society and state, but both won adherents in spite of persecution, and questions of reform were raised by both.

Immediately someone will object that some analogies are artificial, or strained at the most, and that it would be better to restrict discussion to Islamic times and forget the ancient history. This would be the easiest course to follow, but, in my opinion, it would ignore the continuity of Iranian culture even through the great changes of Islam. One may learn more about Iran by comparing the state-church of the Sasanians with the state-church of the Safavids, than by disregarding all parallels. Let us consider Sasanian ritualism and orthopraxy.

The Sasanian empire which lasted from about AD 226 to

630 was a conscious revival of the Achaemenid state with its pretensions to universality. The Sasanian rulers considered themselves 'king of kings of Iran and non-Iran whose seed is from the gods', as we find in their inscriptions. There was something new in this state, however, and that was an organized church with orthodox dogmas and ritual. The story of the consolidation of the church is out of place here, but once established with its priestly hierarchy, it followed the course of many state churches in history which lost their vigour and became stultified appendages of the government bureaucracy. The picture we have of the Zoroastrian faith at the end of the Sasanian empire is one of a church absorbed by tedious ritual and protocol. Minute observances of everyday life, such as the Zoroastrian way to cut one's fingernails, plus an elaborate fire ritual extending from the ever-burning central fire temples of the realm through provincial fire temples, city, village and home fire altars, kept pious people very occupied. It is no wonder that Islam seemed like a breath of fresh air to many Iranians. It must be confessed too that Sasanian Zoroastrianism does not impress anyone who reads the texts which have survived, with its intellectual or theological content. Much may have been lost but we can only base our conclusions on what has survived.

If we consider the narrow, exclusive ghetto-like mentality of the Zoroastrians later under Islamic rule, however, we may do a certain injustice to Sasanian Zoroastrianism by assuming that it too was just the same as the later faith. The fact that it was under the Sasanids the official religion with imperial support made Zoroastrianism far more concerned with political allegiance to the ruler and with sanctions for the actions of the king of kings, hence with orthopraxy, than it was later under Islam. One might say that Sasanian Zoroastrianism was more concerned with orthopraxy than orthodoxy, while the reverse was true after it had lost state support and become a minority religion under Islam. One may postulate the existence of a certain tolerance in thought under the Sasanians which disappeared among orthodox Zoroastrians under Islam.

A tolerant attitude towards matters philosophical and religious, however, was carried over into Islam by many Zoroastrian savants who converted to the new faith. The enormous contribution to Islam and Islamic thought by Persians is too well known to be catalogued again. It is generally accepted that the 'Golden Age' of the 'Abbasids in the ninth century AD was led, if not dominated, by Persian scholars. The intellectual movement of the free thinkers in this period, called Mu'tazilites, was again sparked by Iranians and undoubtedly contributed much to broadening Islam and making it acceptable to many intellectuals. It is difficult to determine how many Mu'tazilite ideas were absorbed into Shiism, but undoubtedly there was a continuity. Shiism later, however, came to be dogmatic and even hostile to the mystics, although an element of tolerance and liberality is not lacking in orthodox 'twelver' Shiism, the official faith of modern Iran.

A definition of Shiism, itself, must be qualified by reference to various sects within the general designation. Generally speaking, Shiism represents the messianic, personal authoritarian aspect in Islam, exemplified in the figure of the *imam,* the link between Allah and his people on earth. Above we compared Shiite Islam with Christianity and Sunni, or 'orthodox' Islam, with Judaism. Since the Sunnis place their faith in the Qur'an, the holy word of God, or in the Law like the Jews, the above analogy would seem more appropriate than the frequent comparison of Shiite-Sunnis with Roman Catholic and Protestant Christianity. In a sense Shiism has a hierarchy akin to Catholicism but with less emphasis on scriptural dogma than the Sunnis. The comparisons with the two branches of Christianity are difficult. Furthermore, in origin Christianity is a Jewish sect, as Shiite Islam could be called a sect of Sunni Islam.

The Arab political origins of Shiism do not concern us here, but the figures of the son-in-law of the prophet, the Caliph

'Ali, his son Husain, and his descendants are the saints of Shiite Islam, the guides to the perplexed throughout succeeding generations. The last, or twelfth *imam* in descent from the prophet disappeared and is the hidden *imam* or the coming messiah in the official religion of Iran. In his absence the religious leaders of Shiite Islam known as *mujtahids* direct the people on behalf of the hidden *imam*. In the fullness of time the twelfth *imam* will return and bring justice to the world.

Shiites are also divided into several sects, the most prominent of which is the Ismaili community, the followers of the Aga Khan. For them there is no twelfth hidden *imam* since they follow a different line of descent after the seventh *imam* in the series, Ismail, whence their name. They believe that the *imamate* descended from father to son continuously down to the present young Aga Khan, Karim, who is the spiritual leader of Ismailis in India, Pakistan and East Africa with few followers left in Iran. During the Middle Ages, however, the Ismailis were a dreaded force in Iran known to the Western world as the Assassins with their leader, the 'old man of the mountains'.

The activities of the Assassins represent a feature of Iranian religious life, fanaticism, albeit found elsewhere in the Islamic world. Sometimes also built upon a kind of fanaticism are the secret society, the dervish order, or the club called *anjuman* in Persian. Such societies as the modern *Fedayan-i Islam*, the Muslim fanatics, seem always to have been present in the history of Iran, and at times their influence has been very great. The secret societies should not be confused with dervish orders although the two may overlap.

Dervish orders have flourished in Iran since early Islamic times, sometimes more sometimes less. Their character has also changed, and one might trace their origins back to the pre-Islamic period or even to the time of the Aryan invasions. Indeed some sociologists have argued that such religious orders are present in most religions and found at all times.

Perhaps societies of young men at the dawn of history may be counted as prototypes of the later dervish orders. For our purpose it is sufficient to realize that such organizations have been an important factor in Iranian society for centuries. At the present such dervish orders as that founded by Safi 'Ali Shah, confidant of Nasr al-Din Shah in the nineteenth century, the order of Nimatallah Vali at Mahan in Kirman province, of Salih 'Ali Shah at Behdukht in Khurasan, the Khaksariyya among the Kurds, and many others, are comparable to the Rotary Club or the Elks in the West. Religion, however, is far more pervasive in Iranian life even today, than in the secularized Occident and the dervish orders are a manifestation of the persistence of interest in the spiritual in an ever growing materialistic world.

The mass of the populace in Iran is still concerned with what may be termed folk religion, saint worship, magic and charm, and the like. This may be seen in the various rites and practices which have as much to do with Islam as say the Christmas tree with Christianity. For example, on the last Wednesday before the new year, which begins on March 21st, Persians make fires and jump over them reciting verses. This use of fire must be a survival from pre-Islamic times. The important new year's holidays, beginning with the first day of spring, the vernal equinox, are pre-Islamic in inspiration. Pilgrimages to holy places, such as the great shrines of Mashhad and Qum are an important feature of popular Shiite Islam and the *imamzadehs* or tombs of the children of the *imams* are found all over the country. Many such shrines were Zoroastrian shrines transformed into Islamic places of pilgrimages with appropriate changes of names. Just as in other faiths, so in Shiism intercession of the saint and miracles may result from pilgrimages to and prayers in holy places. It is impossible here to discuss the many and fascinating features of folk religion in Iran, but religion in all possible phases, from highly intellectual philosophies to crass superstitions not only exists but flourishes in Iran today.

An important part of religion in Iran is the 'church'. Although there is supposed to be no church structure in Islam, the Shiites do have an organization and a hierarchy. The nature of Shiite Islam almost presupposes an organization which takes care of people until the hidden *imam* or messiah returns. The organization and influence of the Shiite 'church' in Iran is most interesting, often misunderstood, and often unknown to both foreign investigators and Westernized Iranians of the upper classes. It is not an open, recorded hierarchy of established ranks and categories. Rather the 'church' is a brotherhood of the learned—those who have studied religion. While the formal organization of the 'church' is quite loose, this does not mean that the religious leaders are disunited, weak or purposeless. Just as with an individual sometimes self discipline is far stronger than rules imposed from outside; so in the 'church' of Shiism the internal strength is far greater than one would believe from the outside. The headquarters of the Shiite faith at the present time are in the town of Qum to the south of Tehran, where there is also a college or university for training religious leaders or *mullahs* who will function as village priests throughout the land. A *mullah* who devotes himself to further study and becomes learned in one or more branches of Islamic learning such as *fiqh* (scholastic jurisprudence), or *kalam* (theology) may become a *mujtahid* if he is accepted by the already established *mujtahids*. A *mujtahid* does not exist in Sunni Islam, for he has the right to give his own interpretations of religious problems, always in conformity with Shiite traditions. This cannot be done in legalistic Sunni Islam where the law books of the four orthodox schools are closed and not subject to addition or amendment. The *mujtahids* in Iran have great prestige and influence not only among their lesser colleagues but also among the populace at large.

Individuals, however, vary considerably in their ideas of propriety and right and wrong, and *mujtahids* are no exception. There are both liberal and reactionary religious leaders and

differences of opinion among them make Shiite Islam peculiarly appropriate for Persians. One cannot exclusively praise or
condemn the religious leaders of Iran and the range of thought
from the sublime to the ridiculous is ever present. The head
of the Shiite world, now called *al-uzma,* is elected by the
mujtahids from among their number, and he is usually the
most respected and distinguished if not the oldest. The late
leader, Ayatullah Burujirdi who died in 1961, was the first
to take an active interest in the outside world by sending
representatives to Washington, D.C. and elsewhere to study
at first hand the Occident. He also started a new mosque
shrine in Qum, built with the traditional Persian tiles. It is
reputed to be the largest mosque compound in the world. At
present his successor has not been determined.

The *mullahs* in Iran have gained a bad reputation among
the Westernized intellectuals for venality, greed and fanaticism
but the conflict between the intellectuals and the traditional
conservatives is the burning problem of Iran today and in-
evitably brightness and light are not all on one side. The
religious leaders feel that the immorality of the comparatively
wealthy, Westernized Persian is reflected in his lack of respect
for Shiite Islam, hence for Iran as well. The two almost
distinct worlds may be seen in the city of Tehran where, north
of Sipah Avenue to the suburb of Shimran and beyond, the
Persian élite have their business establishments or make their
homes, while south of the avenue, in the old city, one passes
from depressed neighbourhood to slum. Because the *mullahs*
are bitter about the upper classes, and because they claim to
be the voices of the masses, they are feared and disliked by
the upper classes. The separation is so pronounced that one
might say that in Iran there is a country within a country or
a state within a state. The government of his imperial majesty,
the shahinshah, rules Iran, but inside is another state, a
theocracy, ruled from Qum. In a village one may find
gendarmes, or officials representing Tehran, but also a *mullah*
and his friends representing Qum. The two groups generally

co-operate but in a clash one cannot predict which would prevail. In conclusion, it must not be forgotten that the *mullahs* are ordinary Persians who have studied religion, hence they reflect the mores of the people from whom they came. It is common to hear the Westernized Persians blame the *mullahs* for all of modern Iran's ills and *vice versa*. Both groups are Persian and represent their country.

To see how the *mullahs* became powerful we turn to the beginning of the modern history of Iran, the rise of the Safavid dynasty and the state-'church' union.

CHAPTER VI

Half the World is Isfahan

RUGS, cats and Shah 'Abbas are the symbols of Safavid Iran where a certain finesse dominates the arts and crafts and indeed life in general. Under the Safavids the disruptive forces of the preceding centuries of Mongolian and Turkish rule were subdued and welded into the new structure which we may call modern Iran, at least in comparison to the millennia of history which the land had already known. We have already mentioned the legacy of Turkish and Mongolian offices and influences in Safavid Iran. The early history of the state from 1524 to about 1560 was occupied with civil wars between various Turkish Qizilbash tribes, each seeking to dominate Shah Tahmasp, successor of Isma'il the founder. The power of the Qizilbash was broken by the introduction of Georgian and Circassian units into the Safavid army in the last years of Tahmasp.

One may profitably draw a parallel between the formation of the Safavid state and that of the Ottoman empire. The co-existence of a religious and a political institution in both, and the forging of a new allegiance and a new government in both, are striking. Both empires, if they may be so called, arose from Turkish military states, but the élite corps of each army came to be based in great part on non-Turkish, even mostly Christian, professional guards, the Janissaries in the Ottoman Empire and the Georgians in the Safavid realm. In both states the governmental bureaucracy operated side by side with a church organization. In the Ottoman empire the Shaykh al-Islam in Istanbul performed 'spiritual' functions on behalf of the caliph-sultan, while under him was a kind of hierarchy of *muftis* 'judges', *khwajas* 'teachers' (Turkish *hoca*) and others. In the Safavid empire by the time of Shah 'Abbas the original missionary zeal, or one might better say the inquisition, was over since Shiism had become dominant and was the religion of the state. Consequently the early religious figure called the *sadr* whose primary task was to impose doctrinal unity, and to root out heresy, had given way to the *mujtahid* who was more concerned with learning, though in a medieval, scholastic manner. With the establishment of a Shiite state, learned men of this persuasion from all over the Muslim world came to Iran such that it became the centre of Shiite learning. On the other hand, many Shiite missionaries went from Iran to Moghul India and elsewhere so Iran was not totally isolated from the rest of the Islamic world.

There is no space to catalogue the religious teachers of the Safavid period or their teachings. The philosophical writings of Mir Damad (d. *ca* 1631) and Mulla Sadra of Shiraz (di *ca* 1641) have been characterized by some scholars as the bases on which the movements of Babism and then Bahaism were built, but this is a matter of much dispute. It is rather the popular theological writings of such prolific Shiite divines as Muhammad al-'Amili (d. 1622) and Muhammad Baqir-i Majlisi (d. 1700) which set the tenor of the age. Their writings seem rather dull and even turgid today, but in their time they dealt with problems troubling the common folk as well as the intellectuals. The necessity for an *imam* to lead the Muslims and the belief in the hidden *imam* were elaborated in teachings which laid the doctrinal basis for a Shiite 'church'. In the time of the later Safavids the *mujtahids* or learned men of Shiite Islam gained a strong place in Persian society, which position has been challenged only recently, primarily by the impact of the West.

It is significant to remember that Iran did not have the same history of learning as the Arab world which produced no great thinker after Ibn Khaldun at the end of the fourteenth century. For the Sunni Muslims all that was important in thought, and especially in philosophy, had been said by the Sunni theologians, and like the dependence of medieval Western Europe on Aristotle, there was no incentive to question past masters. The story of Islamic philosophy in Iran was different than that of the Arab world and the Ottoman Empire, since various schools flourished and competed in Iran while among the Arabs and Turks one unquestioned orthodoxy in philosophic thought continued in unbroken tradition down to the present.

Scholastic philosophy or theology (*kalam*) was always taught everywhere in the Islamic world, Iran included. Another school of thought, which we might term the peripatetic (*masha'i*), declined in the Arab world after it had been attacked by the great theologian al-Ghazzali, or Algazel as he was called in Europe, early in the twelfth century. It was revived in Iran, however, a century later by Nasir al-Din Tusi, who exalted the role of reason in spiritual knowledge and in salvation. A third school, called the illuminationist or the *Ishraqi*, combining reason and intuition, was founded by a thinker called Suhrawardi and had many adherents in Iran. Finally, the purely mystical, or Sufi philosophy, based on gnosis (*'irfan*) always was popular among the Persians. These four schools of thought continued to flourish in Iran in Safavid times when Mulla Sadra tried to synthesize all of them into a unified philosophy. So creative philosophical thought continued to be manifest in Iran long after it seemingly had ceased elsewhere in the Islamic world.

Thus Iran has had a continuous and developing philosophical tradition from at least the tenth century of our era which cannot be matched by the Arabs or Turks. How much this has influenced the common people is difficult to say, but probably more than generally has been realized in the West, for the Persians greatly respect knowledge and the search for it. The Safavid period of Iran's history is not only one of artistic splendour but also of religious and philosophical development. This period also saw the expansion of forms of state and government.

It is not our intention to discuss the bureaucracy or even changes in offices and titles in Safavid Iran for such an investigation would require too much space. One problem in the study of Persian sources not only of the Safavid, but of all periods of Iran's history, is the confusion, as well as the changes in significance, in titles. For titles of offices are frequently confounded with honorifics and even with personal names. In the Safavid period we find the title *I'timad al-Daula* 'support of the state', in origin an honorific but used in place of the name of the person who functioned as a prime minister. In recent years the 'name' Qavam al-Sultaneh, Prime Minister of Iran after World War II, comes to mind. In the religious sphere the appellative 'Shaykh al-Islam' is likewise in the name-title-honorific category. Suffice it to say that the protocols in, and the organization of, the government and society in Safavid times were complex, excessive in unnecessary ponderosity, and ultimately decadent.

The Safavid state started as a kind of theocracy but became an absolute monarchy, though frequently power resided more in the hands of favourites or relatives than in those of the shah. And just as in the Achaemenid empire, where the *satrap* or governor modelled his court after that of the king of kings, so the high officials of state and the provincial governors of the Safavids copied their sovereign. The shah was himself theoretically a slave of the hidden *imam;* the governors were slaves of the king, and village elders were slaves of the governors. So tyranny over underlings and obsequiousness towards superiors became the pattern of life for all Persians. Those subjects of the shah, such as Afghans in the east and Kurds in the west who did not conform to the elaborate rituals of protocol, were dismissed as benighted barbarians, while foreigners were beyond the pale.

To turn to the life of the people, we find a sharp difference between the townsman and the villager, a division which is still outstanding. Opposition between the city and the country is, of course, not limited to Iran or to Islam, but in the empire of the lion and the sun the peasants had a hard time. The peasants, at the bottom of the totem pole of society, were called *ra'iya*, meaning originally cattle or chattel. The modern term *dihqan* is in its origin a word meaning a landed noble, but the decline of the small landowner class in Seljuk and Mongol times, when military fiefs reduced many landlords to the semi-servile peasant class, caused the reduction in the sense of the word.

To even attempt to survey the chaotic land ownership and taxation systems of pre-Reza Shah Iran would be impossible, and the many and varied abuses in tax collecting in the country would indeed tax the imagination of the reader. Generally speaking, the central government only knew what revenues were expected from the governor of a province, while he knew only what the district officers were to provide him, and so it went down to the peasant. The real amounts of money collected and the sources which ultimately paid were known only to the official in charge of his area. What happened far above or below him was not his concern. James Morier, writing of the early Qajar perior, described the general corruption, and, in passing, he wrote, 'while the business of each individual is to amass money by every possible expedient and particularly by the obvious one of plundering all those unfortunately subjected to his power, no amelioration in these parts can take place.[1] By the end of Reza Shah's reign, it should be said, some order had been introduced into taxation and land owning, but abuses were rife and there were no standard procedures and no recourse for justice.

Generally speaking one can at present divide land holdings in Iran into either landlord (usually absentee) or peasant proprietorship, not to mention public or state land. In all cases the village is the organization which determines and regulates peasant holdings, which in turn are determined by

[1] *A Second Journey through Persia* (London, 1818) 173.

water rights and land subject to cultivation. The family, with its head or elder, is still the basis of society as it was several millennia ago, but in authority the village has taken the place of the ancient clan or of the tribe. Communal responsibility was typical in the past and it fitted in well with the military fiefs of Mongol and of Safavid times when generals were granted fiefs of many villages by the shahs. Again local conditions, the need for irrigation, and other factors, make generalizations about land ownership and taxation in the past somewhat hazardous. In later Safavid and Qajar times, however, the old military fief holder changed into the absentee landlord owning sometimes hundreds of villages, and this is still prevalent, even though many of the old landed aristocracy have been replaced by wealthy city merchants. We shall return to the peasant when speaking of Reza Shah.

The city dweller had a higher standard of living than the peasant, and he usually had a contempt for his rural brother. Islam perhaps favoured an urban over a rural culture and in Iran urbanization had been consciously promoted by the Achaemenids and the Sasanians as it was by the Safavids. Although the city was still in many respects better organized than the village, it seemed to be little more than a collection of villages, each section of the city having almost a separate life of its own. Invariably surrounded by walls, as indeed were most villages too, the Persian city was an interesting part of society.

Authority in the city was exercised at two levels, that of the government and that of the guilds or societies. The overall administration of law and justice was in the hands of civil servants, including the police, as well as religious officials who presided over law courts and the mosques which were centres of social activity. Underneath were craft guilds and other organizations sometimes identical with or overlapping the dervish orders. Using the word 'guild' in its widest sense which is the proper usage for Iran, the individual found his place and his security in society by being a member of such an organization. The guilds developed from early Islamic times, but their real period of growth was during the era of Mongol and Turkish disorders when the Caliphate was ended (in 1258) and central government all over the Near East suffered a setback. Into the vacuum came local organizations such as guilds and religious fraternities and they lasted down to the present.

Certain traditional usages developed in each guild over the centuries. On the whole the guilds were remarkably independent, like miniature states within the larger state. Some of the purposes of a craft guild were to organize and protect the work of craftsmen, to set standards and recruit members. In the general pattern of medieval society everywhere membership in the guilds was hereditary, though one should not blindly equate the Islamic guilds with their European counterparts. Individuals were subject to the discipline of the guild but they were not immune from arrest by the police, or control by government officials. The guilds were also tax collecting agencies, and quotas were assigned to them by the government, while individual levies were made by the head of the guild. The chieftainship was usually hereditary although theoretically, and actually in many cases, he was elected. The head of the guild was the administrator and the arbiter of internal disputes. Obviously over the course of time the relations between guilds and government, as well as inter-guild relations, became complex with many rules and customary procedures.

One great difference between Iran and the Ottoman Empire was the absence of a Levantine class in the former. While certain professions were concentrated in the hands of Jews or Armenians in Iran, there was no large group such as the Levantines, the mixed families of the Ottoman Empire usually Jewish or Christian, who ran the business of the Empire. In the Ottoman Empire Turks were soldiers and bureaucrats, not merchants or craftsmen. In Iran, on the other hand, the Persians were active in all domains, including trade, and Persian merchants were busy all over the Near East holding their own with the Levantines, or even with Hindu merchants in India. The caravanserai was a characteristic feature of Iranian trade and commerce, found usually on the outskirts of cities or villages.

To return to the city, each guild had its own quarters, frequently just an extension of the bazaar. For example, the shoemakers or the brass workers would have a bazaar where all shops of that craft were located, behind which were their living quarters, their mosque and their special bath houses. Industry, of course, until recently was on the craft level, and textiles generally represented the leading industry.

It must be emphasized that down to the reign of Reza Shah, and indeed to the present, most of the towns as well as the countryside were little touched by significant changes in the capital and life continued much as it had for centuries. Perhaps the greatest material change for all the people was brought by the discovery of oil in southern Iran in 1908. The process by which the camel gave way to the motor car and the caravanserai to a garage is well on the way to completion, and petroleum products have penetrated even to isolated villages. Undoubtedly the next few generations in Iran will see even more changes in the land and people, but vestiges of the past will not have vanished completely.

We have mentioned the bazaar and this perhaps more than any other feature of Iranian, or Near Eastern, society has intrigued the foreigner, especially the tourist. The bazaar, as we have seen, was more than just a market place for the manufacture and sale of goods; it was a world unto itself. Most general books on Iran tell of the character of the bazaar, how news travels like wildfire, and how the bazaar can exercise influence on the government by closing, or by organizing mobs. It has been described as a viable organization which was the prime expression of the old way of life. It did provide a framework for society, a means of expression against governmental tyranny and the like. In the city the bazaar had, in a sense, replaced the ancient clan or tribal loyalty of the urban

Persian as the village had done similarly for the villager, although, of course, among the nomads the old vertical loyalty of family, clan, tribe, and nation was still the only one. For the settled and especially the town Persian, loyalty complex of family, guild, bazaar, and city had replaced the older *'asabiyya*. With the breakdown of guild and bazaar, and the new mobility with automobile and train, the city loyalty is now also vanishing. One may suggest that this is one of the dilemmas of present day Iran—that a new *'asabiyya* has not been found or created to replace the old, which vanishes as the pillars of the old society crumble.

It must be said that city or provincial loyalty was quite strong, generally throughout the Islamic period of Iran's history. It not only extended to personal names, whereby a man would take the name of his city as a distinguishing mark but also to a civic pride, most marked when he was abroad. Thus we have the famous philosopher al-Rhazes from medieval Rayy just outside the site of present Tehran. Certain cities had certain specialities in the arts, in cuisine, or in other matters. For example, in confectionaries today Qum is noted for its special sweets *sohan*, similar to peanut brittle; Isfahan is famous for *gaz*, a nougat, while Yazd has many such specialties. The rugs of Kirman, like the cats, are distinctive, and in wool and craftsmanship probably the best in Iran, although rug makers of Kashan, Tabriz and elsewhere would dispute this. Shiraz has the appellation *dar al-'ilm* 'abode of knowledge'; Qum is called *dar al-aman* 'house of refuge', and so on. Much has changed in Iran but city particularism is one of many things which is changing only slowly after the momentous reforms of the Reza Shah period.

Half the world is Isfahan, goes a saying, and that city, in the heart of Persia, evokes the glory of the Safavid age with its beautiful mosques and bridges, the imperial carpets, miniatures and tile work. But Isfahan today is a centre of the textile industry, mainly developed during the reign of Reza Shah, and it is called the Manchester of Iran. In this city one should be able to assess the impact of a Westernized factory system of production on the populace. The industrialization of Isfahan, however, is mostly limited to textiles, and the embryonic growth of labour unions and problems of industrialization have had little effect on the mass of the people. Until a greater spread of industrialization in other fields occurs, the textile machines are taken into the culture of Isfahan with a minimum of disrupting factors. There is now no significant industrial proletarian class in Iran, but the future may bring such a development.

There are many facets of daily life in Persia which help to explain the Persian and his country today, but we cannot discuss them here. The abject poverty of thousands of his countrymen is frequently unknown to, or ignored by, the Westernized, intellectual Persian of the upper classes. The common medicine, the aspirin of the masses in the past, has been opium, and since the poppy is grown in quantity in Iran it is readily available. The curse of opium, as well as *shire,* the dregs of opium, lies heavily on the people although legal prohibitions are reducing their use. Also in some oasis villages of the central deserts one may encounter almost grown children who have never tasted meat, and who survive mainly on sunshine and bread. In the same area are lead and copper mines where young children work since they are sufficiently small to be able to crawl into small tunnels to obtain the ores. The tiny fingers of children can weave some of the fine Persian carpets better than adults with larger hands. Whether this is today the rule or not in mining and weaving is difficult to say, but child labour is surely still widespread. So half the world is Isfahan, and the other half is poverty, sickness and escape from the troubles of this world in the fumes of an opium pipe.

CHAPTER VII

The Overdeveloped Occident

MOST scholars support the contention that Iran, the Near East and the Orient suffered a decline in the seventeenth, eighteenth and nineteenth centuries and were rescued from collapse by the impact of the West. It has even been asserted that Islam was completely dormant from the twelfth until the twentieth century. Such generalizations, as usual, have an element of truth in them, but they invariably have as a background the view of European history which had a golden age under the Greeks, a decline under the Romans, the Dark Ages and then the Renaissance. The history of Iran, and generally the Near East, is interpreted in relation to the European viewpoint. We have seen that the high point of recent Persian history was the Safavid period with a subsequent decline in the eighteenth century. The decline, however, was more cultural and perhaps spiritual than political, although the political or military fortunes of Iran fluctuated from a low point during the Afghan occupation of Isfahan from 1722 to 1729, to a high point in the sacking of Delhi in 1739 by Nadir Shah.

If we analyse the eighteenth and nineteenth centuries of Iran's history from an internal rather than from an external position with reference to European history, the decline seems normal and not unexpected. During the Safavid Empire the principles of orthodox Ja'fari or Twelver Shiism were well and exhaustively established. Canons of literature had been frozen as well as principles of art and the crafts. The apogee had been passed and one could only try variant themes on the masterpieces. Once a culture achieves perfection, or what the people believe to be the highest state of their development, there is only one way to go, down. All that was necessary to be said had been said in an incomparable fashion; all that was to be created had already been made with inconsummate skill. One could only hope to emulate. But this was normal and has been often repeated in human history. What was not normal in world history was the Renaissance in Europe followed by the Enlightenment in the eighteenth, the scientific explosion of the nineteenth century, and the twentieth century of one universe—of course a Western one. The burden of explanation rests not on the historian of the so-called underdeveloped countries, but on the historian of the super-developed Occident. That is what is unusual, but, of course, all depends from what point one views world history.

The Afghan invasion of Iran was the consequence of the weakness of the later Safavid state, a weakness in the spiritual and cultural as well as the purely military sphere. The despotism of the shahs, the horde of sycophants at court, as well as harem intrigues, could not fail to affect the general population. The eighteenth century in Iran, in spite of the victories of the conqueror Nadir Shah (1736-1747), and the relatively benevolent rule of Karim Khan Zend (1750-1779) over the land from his capital of Shiraz, was a time of disintegration. Not only did the fallen tiles from the buildings of Shah 'Abbas remain on the ground, but the ravages of war, famine and pestilence caused a significant shift in the social organization of the Iranians. The disintegration of governmental authority brought a corresponding strengthening of the 'vertical' order of society—the family, clan and tribe. One might call the eighteenth and even nineteenth centuries in Iran after the old Arabic designation of the Parthian period of Iran's history, the *muluk al-tawaif,* or the period of 'the tribal kings'. Reza Shah ended this period, but important vestiges of it, as well as of the more distant past, are still with the Persians today.

Some people claim that culture flourishes and burns even brighter in times of troubles, and there may be some justification for the Toynbeean challenge-response theory of history, but in the case of Iran it was a question of life or death, rather than merely of activity or quiet study in a retreat, and this question was determined by peace and order or war and violence. Europe was never a marginal oasis culture as Iran, so the different circumstances in this case cannot be fruitfully compared.

The nineteenth century in Iran brought a new dynasty of the Turkish tribe of Qajars founded by a eunuch, Aga Muhammad. It also brought the West into close contact with Iran, and made of Iran a pawn in great power politics. Contacts between Iran and the West were, of course, much older than the nineteenth century, but we may begin with the Safavids.

The age of discoveries, of European expansion around the world also brought Europeans to Iran. In the sixteenth and seventeenth centuries Roman Catholic missionaries and a few merchants came from Europe to Safavid Iran. Their respective purposes were to evangelize, in which they were not very successful, and to open trade, wherein they were better rewarded.

The enterprising English East India Company was successful in obtaining from Shah 'Abbas the right to open 'factories' or centres of trade in Iran. An English ambassador was sent to Isfahan and factories were opened in Shiraz and in Isfahan in 1617. Trading privileges were advantageous for the Company and the shah was happy to secure the aid of the English in ousting the Portuguese from the Persian Gulf. The port of Bandar 'Abbas became the headquarters of the English merchants after the capture of the nearby Portuguese held island of Hormuz. In popular parlance the old name of the port continued to be used though the English corrupted this into Gombroon, and so it appears in many English official documents.

The Dutch East India Company by the middle of the seventeenth century had succeeded in almost replacing the British.

The latter, however, did continue precariously in the face of heavy competition and later, because of developments in Europe, the Dutch and the British composed their differences in the Persian trade, in face of a common rival France.

French influence in Persia really started with the Capuchin monks who established a mission in Isfahan in 1628. Frenchmen were also found among the Carmelites and Jesuits established in Iran. For them trade was at first a private affair. In 1664 under Louis XIV France too established an East India Company, but this company never held the same position, or reaped such profits, as did its Dutch or English counterparts. On the other hand the tenacity of individual Frenchmen in maintaining residence in Isfahan and elsewhere through troubled times, and spreading French culture, is a feature of French foreign relations to this day. Although the British and Dutch feared French trade competition it did not materialize. Instead posterity has a series of entertaining books about the trials and tribulations of French envoys to Persia and those of Persian ambassadors to Paris, in which romance has more than a passing share of interest.

Although unofficial Russian missions had come to Iran previously, the first large embassy came in 1664 from Tsar Alexis Mikhailovich to Shah 'Abbas II. It accomplished little save to rouse some ill will. The accession to the throne of Muscovy of Peter the Great changed the relations between the two countries, hitherto mostly concerned with trade which was in the hands of Armenian merchants. The Russian urge to the East was actively promoted by Peter who probably dreamed of using the Caspian Sea as a route to Central Asia and India. Several expeditions explored and mapped the Caspian Sea coasts, but the main diplomatic move came in 1697 when a Russian ambassador arrived in Isfahan with several requests, among them a plea to declare war against the common enemy the Ottoman Turks. Nothing came of this and Peter was too occupied in warfare with the Swedes to turn to Persia. A second mission in 1717 accomplished as little as the previous one.

The Afghan occupation of Isfahan gave both the Russians and the Ottomans a chance to interfere in Persian affairs, the former ostensibly as protector of the Christians in the shah's domains and the latter in a similar capacity for the Sunni Muslims. The Russians took Baku in 1723 while the Turks moved into western Iran on a number of fronts. The treaty of July 8, 1724 between Russia and the Ottoman Empire divided much of western Iran between the two powers. Russia obtained Daghestan, including Derbend and Baku, Gilan and Mazanderan, while the Turks took over Georgia, Shirvan, Azerbaijan and Kurdistan. The treaty, which prevented a war between Turkey and Russia, was a presage of similar partitions much later. The Russians claimed they were acting in support of the Safavid dynasty against the Afghan usurper, but the fevers of the jungle lowlands so decimated Russian troops stationed in the Caspian provinces, that the remnants were only too glad to leave in 1725 after Peter the Great's death.

The scene was changed by the appearance of Nadir Khan, whose rise to fame resembles that of Reza Shah in many ways. He became a great general who cleared the Afghans and the Ottomans from Persian soil, while by the treaty of Resht in 1732 Russia gave up claim to all lands south of the Kura River in Transcaucasia. Nadir who became shah in 1736 not only reconquered territory which had been lost to Persia but invaded India, Turkistan and Daghestan where he successfully installed governments to his own liking, while the island of Bahrain and large parts of Mesopotamia submitted to Persian rule. The assassination of Nadir Shah in 1747 brought an end to the last great expansion of Iran by force of arms, and disunity became the rule even after the Qajars subdued the country. For loyalty was more to the office of shah than to the persons of the Qajar dynasty.

While the eighteenth century was one of great turmoil in Iran, all over the Islamic world there grew the beginnings of protest at the decadence and stagnation of Islamic society. The most famous protest movement was the puritanical sect of the Wahhabis in Arabia but many dervish orders also served as vehicles of similar sentiments. Thus there was an uneasiness and a discontent about the state of affairs in the Near East even before the impact of the West.

Just as the United States 'discovered' the Near East after World War II, so Western Europe first really entered the area in the time of Napoleon. The French Revolution and Napoleon not only marked a great change in Europe but also in the Near East. Perhaps if Napoleon had not invaded Egypt Iran, as well as the Ottoman Empire, might have kept out of European great power politics for a longer period. But Napoleon brought scientists and scholars to Egypt as well as soldiers and the result was the rise of Muhammad 'Ali and the development of modern Egypt under French influences. Iran was far away but French plans for further conquests from their base in Egypt, even to India, included support from the Qajar dynasty. French missions to Iran were matched with British and Russian counter moves and Iran was drawn into the conflicts of European powers.

It was almost inevitable that Russia and Iran would clash in Transcaucasia since the conflict of interests there was acute. The Georgian monarchy had placed itself under Russian protection but the Qajars considered Georgia a part of their domains. In 1795 the Persians sacked Tiflis causing great destruction and slaughter. Russia's 'manifest destiny' both as an imperialist power, as well as champion of the Christian peoples of Transcaucasia, primarily the Georgians and Armenians, was not to be denied, and in two wars with Persia the Russians won easy successes mainly because of the incompetence of the Persian officers. The treaties of Gulistan in 1813, and especially of Turkomanchai in 1828, fixed the northern border of Iran along the Aras River and established commercial relations and extra territorial rights for Russians in Persia. The treaty of Turkomanchai, however, marked a turning point in Iran's history, and further it set the pattern for all future European relations with Iran. Turkomanchai inaugurated the nineteenth century in Iran, and just as the nineteenth century in Europe begins with Napoleon and ends with World War I, so in Iran it really begins with Turkomanchai and ends with Reza Shah Pahlavi.

Until Turkomanchai many Europeans, as well as the Persians, held to the illusion that Iran was a great power. Had not ambassadors from all sides tried to secure alliances with the Safavids and with the Qajar Fath 'Ali Shah? Had they not sought to sway the 'shadow of Allah on earth' and his ministers with gifts and promises just to secure his good will? But the reality was something different. Before Turkomanchai Iran was an independent country courted by England, France and Russia. After 1828 it was clear that Iran was a weak power, its very survival dependent on Russian goodwill and British counter support. Just as over two thousand years previously the Persians had learned how to bribe the Greeks, now the Europeans discovered the ease with which the shah and his courtiers could be bought.

Persian efforts to recoup their losses in Transcaucasia against a weaker opponent in Afghanistan failed because of British opposition, for both Iran and Afghanistan were destined to serve as relatively inert buffers between the northern bear and the lion in India. Symptomatic of the period is the word of history on Fath 'Ali Shah who died in 1834, and under whom the position of Iran in the world changed so radically. He was known for his extremely long beard, his many children, and his excessive greed. *Vanitas, vanitatum omnia est vanitas* might well be the motto of Iran in the nineteenth century, for most Persians did not realize that times had radically changed.

As one reads the modern history of Iran he is struck time and again with the melancholy possibilities of the preposition 'if', or what might have been. For instance, the crown prince 'Abbas Mirza, governor of Tabriz, in spite of his defeat by the Russians, was an able and progressive person. Because of his efforts, including the dispatch of students to Europe, Tabriz became the most progressive city in Iran and Azeris became especially prominent in Iran's foreign service. Unfortunately the prince died before Fath 'Ali Shah. Also the beginning of the reign of the youthful Nasr al-Din Shah promised to be a period of reform led by the Prime Minister Mirza Taqi Khan, who imitated the Tanzimat reforms of Ottoman Turkey. When Mirza Taqi began to reduce the pensions of the many Qajar princes and to attack the sale of posts and bribery he trod on many toes. If the shah had supported him and turned a deaf ear to his adversaries, much might have been accomplished, but the Prime Minister was removed from office and put to death in 1852.

The interaction of internal discontent with growing foreign influences produced a series of social-religious movements in Iran, the most important of which was that of the Babis. Much has been written about the Babis and their successors the Bahais and we shall but briefly review their history here. 'Ali Muhammad, called the Bab or 'Gate', was born in Shiraz in 1819 of a merchant family. He journeyed to Nejef in Mesopotamia where the young man met a *sayyid* (descendant of the prophet) called Kazem Reshti, head of the Shaykhi sect which believed in the immanent return of the messiah, the hidden, twelfth *imam*. After the death of Kazem in 1843 'Ali Muhammad proclaimed himself the Bab or forerunner of the messiah or *mahdi,* but in 1847 he declared himself the *mahdi* and wrote a book the *Bayan* which became a holy book for his disciples. The Bab, as he is usually called, taught that he had come with a new message for the present age replacing Muhammad and the Qur'an which had replaced Jesus and the Evangiles, which had replaced Moses and the Pentateuch. A new order of society, a new prophet and new laws had now become necessary because the previous system had decayed and had become corrupted. His teachings were in a good Shiite tradition plus new ideas of tax revision, social reform, and the like, in which he was accused of exhibiting old Mazdakite, or other heretical tendencies.

In 1849 and 1850 Babi uprisings occurred in several parts of the country but they were cruelly suppressed, and in July 1850 the Bab himself was executed in Tabriz. New Babi revolts were put down and an unsuccessful attempt on the shah's life brought bloody reprisals. Many Babis fled to the Ottoman Empire and Russia. A split in their ranks occurred and the majority followed the leadership of one Mirza Husain 'Ali, called Baha'ullah. He led the group, now called Bahais, on a new path, emphasizing liberal ideas and thought, primarily of Western Europe, over the Shiite religious elements, such that Bahaism became a universal, cosmopolitan religion with a centre at Haifa, Palestine and with adherents all over the world as well as in Iran. Bahaism still has followers in Iran and it is a potent force for change and reform. The Iranian government has been harsh on the Bahais, usually under the instigation of the orthodox Shiite religious leaders.

Soviet scholars have characterized the Babi movement as a genuine peasant mass movement, but Bahaism becomes for them a bourgeoise, capitalist sect with certain liberal but antiquated religious ideas. Such a simple view is not only scholarly unsound but probably itself is now antiquated in the Soviet Union.

The second half of the nineteenth century in Iran is the story of further decline, of English-Russian rivalry, and of the expansion of European commercial interests in the country. We have already seen how the political position of Iran changed from an independent power to a buffer state. The commercial interests of the foreigners changed from mere trade in textiles and luxury objects to exploitation of natural resources and a mass market for the factories of Europe. This new expansion has been termed economic imperialism and it became of great importance after the discovery of oil by a British company in southern Iran in 1908. Before turning to British-Russian rivalry in the early twentieth century with the

F

rise of nationalism and the Constitutional movement, let us briefly examine the process of contact between the Persians and Europeans which was continuing throughout the nineteenth century.

The Catholic missionaries and schools in Iran were joined by Protestants in the early half of the century. American Presbyterians opened a centre in Urmia, now called Rezaiyeh, in 1834. They later opened schools and hospitals in northern Iran in Resht, Tehran and Mashhad. The Church of England, in agreement with the Presbyterians, concentrated in southern Iran. The influence of these Western charitable institutions in the country was undoubtedly significant since the common folk came in direct contact with foreigners and new ideas. We have noted that the Russians set the pattern for other countries in obtaining special privileges and extraterritorial rights in Iran. In 1856 the United States received the same extraterritorial capitulatory rights in Iran as Great Britain, France and Russia. In 1882 an American Legation was opened in Tehran which had become the capital of Iran under the Qajars. There was little work for the diplomats, however, since American-Persian trade was small and the missionaries generally took care of themselves.

The Persians were not inactive in seeking contacts with the West. A few Persian students were sent to Europe during the reign of Fath 'Ali Shah, and in 1851 the first college on Western lines was founded in Tehran and throughout the century influences from the outside steadily increased. Intellectual ideas, of course, only reached the upper class Persians, although material evidence of the West penetrated to the common folk as well. The Anglican and Presbyterian missionaries worked primarily among the Christian Assyrians and Armenians and brought Western ideas to them, but the latter were not in sufficient numbers in Iran to wield much influence. The minorities, however, did not form a Levantine class as in the Ottoman Empire where the Turks were shielded from contact with Europeans. The religious minorities in Iran,

Assyrians, Armenians, Jews, Zoroastrians, and Bahais took advantage of the benefits of Westernization more than the Muslim majority. Not that Western influence was always beneficial and never baneful. The foreign exploitation of Iran, however, was felt by the court and aristocracy with little reaction among the masses until the turn of the century.

There is no really detailed study yet of the background of the Persian revolution and the Constitutional movement of 1906-1909, but forces were at work which prepared the way for the upheaval. The examples of Arabi Pasha and his literary supporters in Egypt, the work of Jamal al-Din Afghani and the modernist movements in India and in the Ottoman Empire cannot have failed to find some echoes in Iran, although it must be admitted the direct evidence is slight. The interesting features of Iran's revolution are the participation in it of both Westernized intellectuals and conservative traditionalists such as religious leaders and merchants. A foretaste of the power of the clergy-led masses was the reaction of the Persians against a tobacco monopoly which had been given by the shah to a British concern in 1891. The boycott against tobacco was so effective that the monopoly was cancelled. Nonetheless much of Iran's economy by 1906 was run by foreigners.

A British subject, the banker Baron de Reuter in 1872 had obtained an impressive concession from the shah to exploit minerals and oil, construct railways, and a host of other monopolies. It too had to be cancelled, mostly because of Russian pressure, but de Reuter instead received the right to create a bank and in 1889 he set up the Imperial Bank of Persia. Russia had not been idle, and a Russian gained fishing rights in the Caspian in 1888, while the best military force in the country was the Persian Cossack Brigade with Russian officers, created in 1879. Nasr al-Din Shah made two trips to Europe and his diaries are full of interesting observations about his experiences but the voyages cost great sums of money so he, which meant his country, was in debt, hence he allowed the foreign concessions to repay those debts.

The story of the loans of Nasr al-Din and of his son Muzaffar al-Din is one of increasing indebtedness to British or Russian banks until it seemed as though the nation would go bankrupt and into the receivership of the two foreign countries.

People who deplore present conditions in Iran may forget that the country has been in a state of crisis or shock for many of the sixty odd years since the beginning of the century. Present disorder, corruption and weak government are nothing like pre-Reza Shah days. Indeed it is difficult to imagine how the despotic, inefficient court and bureaucracy of the Qajars really functioned. The rise of nationalism and the Constitutionalist movement only served to confuse still further the decrepit medieval government of Muzaffar al-Din Shah.

The activity of Persians outside of Iran, some of them in exile, was extensive in pre-Constitution days. Persian newspapers or journals were published in Calcutta, Cairo, Istanbul, Paris and elsewhere attacking the tyranny of the shah and advocating reforms of the government, although few presented specific plans for a parliament, code of laws, or the like. Perhaps the most important centre of such activity was Transcaucasia for several reasons. First, Russian Azerbaijan was predominantly Shiite like Persian Azerbaijan and many pilgrims from the north visited the Shiite shrines in Iran where contacts with the local population were made. Second, the Azeris were influenced by writings in Turkish and developments in the Ottoman Empire. Finally, the Azeris in both Iran and in the Tsarist empire were more Westernized than their co-religionists. The oil fields of Baku brought Russification more to the Azeris than to other Caucasian Muslims while the position of the Azeris in Iran in respect to modern ideas is well known. Iranian culture was very strong among Caucasian Muslims. So intellectuals in Iran were not unaware of the agitation in writings for change and reform. Yet the Constitution came into existence almost accidentally and unexpectedly, since those who precipitated the crisis which led to the granting of a Constitution by the shah were not the Westernized intellectuals but rather merchants and religious leaders.

The immediate cause of the Constitutional uprising was a protest of some merchants and *mullahs* against the Prime Minister, who was held responsible for the corruption in government and also for the expensive trips of the shah to Europe. They took refuge or *bast,* as the old Persian custom was called, in a mosque in Tehran, and later they moved to a shrine south of the city. The shah promised to dismiss his hated Prime Minister and to institute reforms but as soon as the agitators had dispersed he reneged on his promises and the Prime Minister started on a policy of repression of the discontented merchants and *mullahs.* The result was the famous *bast* in the British Legation compound by about ten thousand Persians. The shah who was sick and dying consented to establish a parliament and a Constitution, and both came into existence before he died in January 1907.

His son Muhammad 'Ali Shah was a despot determined to suppress the Constitution. Ranks were drawn for a struggle between the followers of the shah and supporters of the Constitution, when the infamous, in Persian eyes, Anglo-Russian Agreement of 1907 was announced. In effect it divided the country into two spheres of influence, the Russian in the north and over much of Iran and the British south of Isfahan and in the southeastern part of the country. This treaty shocked many of the Constitutionalists who had hoped for British support against the shah and his Russian advisers. The rapprochement between the Russians and the British, however, might have been forseen, especially after the disastrous defeat of the Tsar's troops by the Japanese in 1905 and the Russian revolution of the same year. The defeat of Russia by the Japanese had a great propaganda effect on the Orient since for the first time a major European power had been defeated by an Oriental state. Furthermore the growing strength of Germany was another factor which brought the Russians and the British together.

It is interesting that the Persian revolution occurred when the country was in effect under a dual foreign protectorate. In June 1908 the new shah ordered the Persian Cossack brigade to bombard the Parliament building. The reaction of the Constitutionalists was quick and perhaps unexpected by the shah. Forces were formed at Tabriz, Resht and Isfahan and the revolution began. There was scattered fighting and Russian troops moved into Tabriz to restore order. The Constitutionalists, however, managed to enter Tehran in July 1909 and depose the shah who took refuge in the Russian Legation. Muhammad 'Ali fled to Russia and the parliament or *majlis* named his eleven year old son Ahmad ruler of Iran.

Fighting was not over since a breakdown in local government had occurred all over the country. The victors in the civil war, as it might be called, quarrelled among themselves dividing into extremist and liberal groups. The chaos in the country induced the ex-shah Muhammad 'Ali to try his luck again; so in 1911 he landed on the south Caspian coast and prepared an expedition against Tehran. His forces were defeated and British diplomatic pressure caused his withdrawal to Russia and permanent exile.

At this time an interesting episode happened when an American economic expert named Morgan Shuster was appointed in 1911 to reorganize the finances of the country. Shuster tried in many ways to increase revenue, to end abuses and to put order into the tax system, but he clashed with the Russians when he tried to apply pressure to rich Persian protegés of Russia. The Tsarist government presented an ultimatum to the Persian government which was forced to dismiss Shuster. The latter returned to America and wrote a book called *The Strangling of Persia,* which translated into Persian became a best seller in the country. Shuster while capable and perhaps idealistic did not understand some of the reasons for the sorry plight of Iran or the necessity for acute diplomatic activity before any course of action was determined.

The Russians became enemies number one in the minds of

the Persians when they bombarded the Shiite shrine at Mashhad ostensibly to make a demonstration in order to protect the lives of Russian nationals in the city. With the breakdown of central government authority in the provinces where bandits proliferated, it seemed to many Persians that Russia would have to assume complete control of the government if Iran was to survive as an entity. Such was the unhappy situation at the outbreak of World War I.

The declaration of war in Europe brought hope to the Persians that their enemies would be defeated by the Central Powers, and one need not wonder why the Germans were popular and received support in Iran. The land of Iran was a theatre of war and Turks fought Russians while German agents roused the Qashqais and other tribesmen against the British, who were vitally concerned to protect their oil installations. On several occasions the Persian government was ready to join the conflict against the Allies but the fortunes of war prevented a hasty decision, such that Iran remained neutral throughout, though her sympathies could not be disguised.

The Russian Revolution and the subsequent withdrawal of Russian troops from Iran left a vacuum into which the British in a desultory manner marched. By the end of the war the British were masters of the country but they did not have the forces or a determined policy to really rule Iran. Nonetheless in 1919 a treaty was proposed which would have placed Iran under British control almost as a protectorate. The Persian people protested in mass demonstrations so the treaty was never ratified by the *majlis*. Bolshevik troops occupied Gilan and it seemed as though the revolution of the proletariat might spill over into Iran. The new Soviet state, however, was too much occupied with internal affairs to concern itself with a revolution in Iran, so the troops were evacuated after the signing of the famous Irano-Soviet treaty of 1921 which for decades remained the basis of relations between the two countries. In that treaty the Soviet Union agreed to end all Persian debts and special Russian privileges in Iran, but the Soviets reserved the right to move troops into the country if they felt threatened by the activities of a foreign power on the soil of Iran. This provided the background for the Soviet invasion of 1941.

Before we turn to Reza Shah we may ask what was the highpoint of the old régime, of Qajar rule in Persian history. The Persian revolution was, in a certain sense, even more significant than the Young Turk revolution in the Ottoman Empire with which it has been compared. In my opinion the Constitution of Iran became the new charisma or 'mystique' for the Persian people in the twentieth century. Just as the mere facts of history do not alone make that history so the Constitution in itself is not as significant as the symbolic meaning, the spiritual value engendered by the fact. The Constitution has become more powerful, for many Persians, than the person or the institution of the shah. It has replaced Muhammad or Shah 'Abbas as the new centre or the new symbol of loyalty, and it has provided a rallying point for a modern *'asabiyya* of the Persians. It now occupies the same, but perhaps even more important position in the minds of many Persians than the Declaration of Independence and the Constitution do in the minds of Americans, and certainly it means far more for the Persians than the Magna Charta does for the English. For this reason alone it would be well to mention several distinctive features of the Iranian Constitution.

The first article of the Constitution states that the official religion of Iran is the orthodox, twelver Shiite sect of Islam, while the second provides for a check on all legislation by religious leaders who will determine whether any decree or law is contrary to Islamic principles. It is an anomaly that the Constitution which was to end despotic government by intro-during liberal ideas, in regard to appointment to high offices more or less insured the opposite. In the days of absolutism, the shah might elevate an Armenian or a Georgian to the highest office in the land, but after the *majlis* came into existence the highest offices in actuality were not open to the ethnic or religious minorities. Unfortunately such was the case with many nascent nationalisms all over the world.

The Iranian Constitution was modelled after the Belgian Constitution and most of its articles, aside from the first two, were really advanced for the Iran of 1906. In spite of religious controls and a few restrictive articles, the Constitution was a remarkable document. If all of the articles had been strictly interpreted and obeyed, Iran would have been a land of relative equality and justice. Unfortunately the translation of fine words into actions sometimes was lacking and laws were ignored. Still the Constitution was a momentous step and a necessary first step in the direction of enlightened government and the development of freedom in Iran.

In the field of foreign relations the British-Russian rivalry dominated the Qajar scene, and even after the Agreement of 1907 the power realities were the same, Russia in Transcaucasia and Central Asia and Britain in India. The shrinking of the world in the twentieth century and the cataclysm of 1914-1918, however, changed not only the old order of politics and society but also the time-honoured rules and principles whereby alliances and power politics were ordered. Many writers about Iran start the modern era with the Constitution, just as in the Ottoman Empire the Young Turk revolution ended the power of a despotic sultan. Yet in both the fruition of those important movements were similar—Mustafa Kemal Ataturk and Reza Shah Pahlavi. Both have been characterized as mere copies of Mussolini or other European dictators who came to power in the post war chaos. Influenced they probably were, but the origins of both the Turkish and the Iranian leader are best sought in the contemporary conditions and in the past of their own lands. In any case the brave new world of Iran began with Reza Shah.

CHAPTER VIII

The End of an Epoch

IT was less than a week before the Soviet-Iranian Treaty was signed in the middle of February 1921 that Reza Khan, a commander of the Persian Cossack Brigade, overthrew the government by a *coup d'état*. Parliamentary government was maintained after a number of arrests had been made, and a new prime minister, Sayyid Ziya al-Din, took office, though actual power resided with Reza Khan. It is impossible to give a biography of the late shah here; perhaps the closest parallel with him would be Peter the Great. Both were impressive by their physical size and the effect they had on those who met them. Both sought to change their people and countries, by violent means if necessary. Both were successful in that Russia after Peter was quite different from what it had been before him and Iran after Reza Shah was never the same.

Reza Khan came to the throne in stages; first he was commander-in-chief of the armed forces and Minister of War. In 1923 he became prime minister and shortly afterwards Ahmad Shah Qajar left for Europe never to return. In 1926 Reza was crowned shah and began a new dynasty which he called after a pre-Islamic word, Pahlavi. What interests us most was his policy of the modernization of Iran, which brought about an upheaval in the society, economy and government of the country, a face-changing operation.

Reza Khan saw early that to bring about reforms one needed force, and so his first task was to increase and reform the army. He had to have the means to enforce his will, in the form of central governmental authority, all over Iran. In 1921 great sums of money from the national budget were allocated for military purposes, and the results of this were not slow in appearing. Reza Khan in 1922 first moved against the openly declared rebels against central authority, and he was successful in securing the allegiance of the Arabs in Khuzistan, and of tribal leaders in Kurdistan. He retook Gilan with its revolutionary government, and soon all of Iran acknowledged the central authority. Reza Khan's main objective in the army was soon achieved in that he created an officer class loyal to him personally. Some young officers were sent to Europe for further training, and foreign advisers were hired to help train the army in Iran. Only a few Swedish officers, however, were directly active in the Iranian army, for Reza Khan wanted to rid his army of all foreign political influence.

After rebels, or opponents outside of Tehran, were crushed or induced to submit, Reza Khan turned to internal opponents, but he was not strong enough to open an attack upon them until he became shah. When he became shah he became 'the shadow of God upon earth' and in this case the shadow of Allah, like Jehovah, was that of a fierce and jealous God. It may appear jaundiced or uncharitable to discuss Reza Shah's reforms under the rubric of opponents whom he had to subdue, but it is more valid to discuss them in this manner than to suppose that Reza Shah had a constructive master plan for the reform and edification of his country.

There were principally two opponents of Reza Shah, the religious leaders and the tribal chieftains. Two other groups in the pattern of power in the country, the great landowners and the merchants, were greatly affected by the new ruler and, while the two might be considered opponents, on the whole they did not really suffer a diminution in their positions. Nonetheless they too may be considered as minor opponents of the sweeping actions of Reza Shah, for they lost certain social privileges. The nobility was by this time dominated by princes of the prolific Qajar royal family. The court protocol and system of prerogatives was changed by Reza Shah, and the honorifics by which many of the nobles were known were abolished. The bases and the instruments of Reza Shah's policy and actions were the army, the gendarmerie, and other agents of central authority. There was a certain amount of confiscation of lands, but since Reza Shah himself became the greatest landowner in Iran by acquiring most of the province of Mazanderan, the foundations of land ownership in the country were little changed.

Many Western writers have attributed the change in Reza Shah in the late thirties, his morbidity, his retreat into seclusion, and his greed, to the removal and execution of his capable Minister of Court, Timurtash, in 1933. Certainly the latter, a polished and even brilliant diplomat, was the contact man between the shah and foreigners, but his virtues have been perhaps too highly sung by the foreigners.

The growth of state monopolies of foreign trade and government control of internal commerce and industry caused much grumbling among the merchants, but in spite of the many restrictions, fortunes were made in commerce during Reza Shah's reign. Although merchants might oppose the shah, they had little power and the government usually had its way.

One of the most spectacular achievements of the régime of Reza Shah was the building of the Trans-Iranian railroad from the Caspian Sea to the Persian Gulf. It was finally finished in 1938 after great engineering difficulties over difficult terrain. While the economic viability of the railroad was and is questionable, undoubtedly its influence on the national morale and the symbolic value of uniting certain provinces with Tehran were enormous. Branch lines planned to Mashhad and Tabriz have been completed only recently. The story of the building of the railroad by representatives of many European countries, yet financed by the Iranian government from its monopolies on sugar and tea, both very important in the national economy, would occupy a book in itself.

Along with the railroad, the new shah built roads, tore down the walls of towns and lifted the urban face of Iran. All this cost great sums and already in 1922 before he became shah, an American economic mission under A. C. Millspaugh came to Iran to reorganize the tax system. During the five years he was in Iran, Millspaugh helped to bring order to the budget and to finances and no doubt he helped greatly to increase the flow of funds to government coffers. As time went on taxes rose and the government entered the realm of production with sugar refineries and factories, matches, shoes, tobacco, glass and many other products, all under state ownership or state control. Even a state tourist agency *Irantour* was created similar to the Soviet Intourist. Private merchants suffered from many of the state monopolies or control over such items as automobile imports and carpet exports. One may say that during the later part of Reza Shah's rule corruption and graft not only increased but took new directions.

The results of the great expenditures and the oppressive taxes could be seen in an embellishment of the cities where money became plentiful, but a corresponding impoverishment of the countryside took place. The shah wanted to make his country independent of the outside world but by entering the path of industrialization he, in fact, tied his country ever more closely to the West, and the country became even more dependent on the West on the economic and industrial side, which was not what he wanted. As a result the demand for luxuries and the necessities of modern living was well on the way to bankrupt the nation.

The struggle with the most powerful and influential opponent probably has aroused more interest in writers on the Reza Shah era than almost anything else. The religious leaders were the custodians of the past and the shah believed that their power had to be broken. Previous rulers had fought with the religious leaders but always within the framework of Islam, and customary law and religious traditions had never been seriously challenged. Reza Shah could not have subdued the clergy had he not had the real support of the army officers and many intellectuals in his attack on the power and influence of religion in Iran. The shah had ostensibly followed the wishes of the Shiite divines in becoming shah instead of establishing a republic on the model of the Turkey of Ataturk, but it was soon clear that Reza Shah would disregard the clergy and run rough-shod over them if they got in his way. His policy of glorification of Iran's pre-Islamic past, substitution of older Persian words for Arabic in the Persian language, and the extolling of the virtues of the Zoroastrians over against the Muslims, was the cultural background of his campaign against Shiite Islam. On the plane of law and authority Reza Shah wrought great changes.

Theoretically in the old days there were three systems of law, two of which might be joined under one heading. One was called 'urf or adat, explained as common law or secular law, and which covered questions such as water rights and land disputes. Since 'urf also concerned the state, one would have expected a mechanism, such as secular courts, to handle cases in non-religious questions. In Iran under the Qajars, however, there was no code or regular administration for 'urf. The second system the shari'ah, as a matter of fact, took over much of the domains which properly should have been reserved to 'urf. The shari'ah courts were religious courts based on the Qur'an and interpreted by mujtahids. The third system, perhaps to be subsumed under 'urf, was that of qanun, or primarily edicts of the shah, usually relating to foreign affairs, taxes, public security, etc.

Although several civil courts were created by the Constitution, such as the Criminal Court and the Court of Appeals, there were no codes or procedures and the shari'ah in fact dominated these courts. Studies had been made and a temporary civil code and a commercial code had been promulgated before Reza Shah. His minister of justice, an exceptionally able jurist called Davar, was able to present a civil code, based mainly on the French civil code, to the *majlis* which approved it in 1928. The foreign capitulations were abolished, and a whole host of new laws relating to the judiciary followed in rapid succession. A law of 1932 required legal transactions to be registered in secular courts, and this more than anything struck at the clergy who had been the custodians of records, from which they had derived much revenue and authority. By a law of December 27, 1936 a further blow was struck at the clergy by requiring all judges to hold a law degree from a secular university or law faculty. Many problems rose from this requirement, but the hold of the religious leaders over the judiciary was broken and by 1940 the *shari'ah* courts had become mere advisory bodies.

Of course some features of *shari'ah* law, especially in personal matters, such as marriages and divorce, were not abrogated but the religious features of them were played down when they were revised. The result is that the present legal structure of Iran is a mixture of modern Western law and traditional Islamic law, while some contradictions or conflicts between the two have been ignored rather than solved. After the abdication of Reza Shah the religious leaders began to recoup influence lost during his reign. Although the real battle with the clergy was fought and won by Reza Shah in the legal domain of the reforms, in the area of religiously sanctioned popular practices changes were less spectacular.

There was promulgated a succession of laws which upset the old order. Licenses were required for the wearing of religious costumes; the popular passion plays during the month of *Muharram* were forbidden; popular dervishes were driven out of towns; religious schools were replaced by secular schools; the veil was removed from women; non-Muslim foreigners were allowed inside mosques, and a new Pahlavi cap was introduced for men as a sign of Westernization. Such social reforms or innovations penetrated to the people and were a manifest example of the power of the shah and his reform government over the forces of tradition led by the *mullahs.* There was opposition and riots had to be suppressed by the troops. Reza Shah himself on one occasion entered the shrine at Qum without removing his boots and personally flogged the *mujtahid* who had dared to criticize the queen for removing her veil. The shah was not averse to using machine guns to restore order to mobs which protested his secular reforms. By the end of the reign of Reza Shah the religious leaders seemed to have been utterly subdued.

Another strong enemy of the shah was the tribe. The tribal leaders never paid more than nominal allegiance to the central government and in the days before the automobile, the aeroplane with a bomb, and the machine gun, they were safe from reprisals in their mountain fastnesses. The tribes had maintained a special pattern of life for centuries moving to the mountains in the summer and migrating to the warm plains in the winter. Such a nomadic life was necessary for the very existence of the tribes since their livelihood, based on sheep, goats and cattle, depended on the availability of forage. Hence any interruption of the seasonal migration spelled disaster for the tribes. Furthermore, large areas of Iran are not suitable for agriculture but only for grazing.

To Reza Shah the tribes were a threat to his authority and to internal security. He determined to force them to settle down and give up their nomadic life. Tribal chiefs were imprisoned, or put to death, and military force was used to subdue the tribes. There were frequent uprisings; for example, the Qashqais revolted in 1929 and again in 1937 but on both occasions were suppressed. The policy of liquidation of the tribes, as the Soviets would say, was only partially successful, for after 1941 the tribes regained much of their lost power.

All groups, landlords, merchants, religious leaders and tribes, were cowed by Reza Shah but they were not by any means destroyed. In one field, however, Reza Shah made incomparable strides, in the field of education of the young. It was apparent to the followers of the shah that unless they educated the children as they thought fit, none of the reforms of the government would ultimately succeed. France provided the model in curricula and in text books, and by the end of the reign of Reza Shah the old *maktabs* or traditional Islamic schools were gone and new modern schools had almost entirely replaced them. Great problems in lack of trained teachers and in equipment made the entire period really one of experimentation in the field of education. The changes from the old system of rote learning of the Qur'an, of Arabic and Classical subjects were almost miraculous. Progressive schools of religious minorities such as the Armenians and Bahais, as well as foreign schools, were brought more and more under the direction of the Ministry of Education. The Zoroastrians, however, for the first time since the Arab conquest of Iran, were favoured because of their relation to the past. The growing nationalism, which was particularly fostered by the officials of the Education Ministry, finally led to the closing of the foreign missionary schools in 1940 and their transformation into public state schools.

In 1935 the corner stone of a new university uniting various existing colleges was laid in Tehran by Reza Shah. Here too French influence was predominant, but the political importance of the student body especially in the ability to organize riots was not felt until after Reza Shah. A very important avenue of Western influence among the educated people of Iran were the Persian students who were educated in Europe or the United States amounting to several thousands every year. Great prestige accrued to the student who had been educated abroad but one problem was almost insuperable, not only in Iran but all over the Orient. This was the reluctance, if not inability, of the educated person to use his hands, for in his own eyes he was an intellectual and could not demean himself by any physical labour. The government of Reza Shah realized that engineers and doctors were needed above all else, yet the faculty of law became the most popular of the faculties since it promised government employment of some kind after graduation and no hand labour. Adult education at nights, the physical education programmes, and many other projects were initiated under the Reza Shah régime. Throughout all of the reforms or development the leading motif was nationalism and glorification of the past.

The nationalism of the Persians frequently led to xenophobia and a feeling of inferiority face to face with foreigners. Of course, similar sentiments were found in various countries after Word War I and they were characteristic of new nationalisms. In the foreign field Iranian nationalism promoted the desire to be independent of any reliance on a foreign power. We have mentioned the end of the capitulatory rights of foreigners in Iran, but the Persian government had to employ foreign advisers, and trade was carried on with Soviet Russia, Britain and at the end of Reza Shah's reign ever more with Germany. Russia and Iran jointly operated the fisheries off the Caspian shores of Iran, especially the caviar industry, while the British operated the oil fields and the refinery at Abadan. Otherwise foreign controlled enterprises in the country were few and unimportant, in marked contrast to Qajar times. In 1933 the shah was successful in obtaining more revenue from the Anglo-Persian Oil Company, but even the increased royalties failed to satisfy the need for more and more funds to continue the modernization of the country. Even with Iran's growing strength Reza Shah did not dare to nationalize the oil industry since Britain would not have tolerated it in those days.

Traditionally in Iran land was the basis of wealth, and by the time of the accession of Reza Shah landholding, water rights and rentals were in a somewhat chaotic state since no survey and registration of land had been done. A beginning was made to register all the land of the country but even today there are large tracts in Baluchistan, the deserts, Kurdistan and elsewhere which are unregistered. Reza Shah's reforms were all from the top down and consequently the peasants were farthest removed from any benefits of the new order. The problem of local authority was pressing, so a law of

December 1935 provided that every village *kadkhuda* or headman was to be invested with a legal, governmental responsibility, although he was not to be elected but to be chosen by the greatest landlord, or, in the case of state lands, to be appointed by the government, which usually meant the local tax and finance office. The *kadkhuda* was not responsible to the people but to the landlord, or the largest property owner if a village had several landlords, and more and more to the government as well. The *kadkhuda* was in charge of affairs relating to agriculture, and he also decided minor disputes, and was in general the liaison man between the owner with the state and the peasants. Established authority was clearly not on the side of the peasant.

Reforms and improvements in agricuture were not very spectacular, and again the landlords, on the whole, profited rather than the peasant, and the greatest landholder of all, the shah, profited the most. He even forbade the cultivation of certain crops such as rice in parts of the country other than Mazanderan where his own estates were. The building of underground tunnels for irrigation, called *qanats,* was encouraged and new seeds and new methods of cultivation were introduced in the country. Again the peasant himself reaped little benefit from any modernization of agriculture. Although there are no statistics, it would seem that large landed estates prospered and grew under Reza Shah while the small owner holdings decreased. Land conditions varied considerably from province to province; for example in Kirman province small land ownership was virtually non-existent since the cost of irrigation by long *qanats* was beyond the means of any village or group of peasants. Usually the independent peasant was in debt and his holding was rarely able to support his family.

One large body of land holding should have suffered dimunition under Reza Shah, the *waqf* or charitable land. The medieval Islamic institution of the endowment (plural *auqaf*), was a kind of foundation, such as has so much proliferated among the wealthy families of modern America.

The Shiite shrine at Mashhad with vast land holdings was probably the largest *waqf* in the country; most of its land, however, was subjected to taxation as other land. Some endowments were taken over by the Ministry of Education, or other agencies of the government, but there is no evidence that religious land declined appreciably in size under Reza Shah.

There were, of course, many tenant farmers in Iran on the large estates. Traditionally the income and expenses on such land were divided into five parts, labour, seed, land, water and draught animals. Actually, conditions varied considerably in different parts of the country. Questions of the yearly distribution of land in a village, the division of crops between landlord and peasant, water rights, and others, are exceedingly involved and cannot occupy us here. Under Reza Shah the position of the peasant certainly declined. Peasants began to flock to the cities, a process greatly accelerated since the departure of Reza Shah, and urban settlement became a serious problem. Even before World War II the jobless peasant in the city formed the nucleus of the city mob which did not express itself until agitators organized the crowds after the abdication of Reza Shah. The absence of health and social services in the countryside was one of many reasons why the peasant was attracted to the city. Perhaps the least of Reza Shah's reform efforts was directed towards improving the peasant and the countryside.

Reza Shah did carry out a monetary revolution in the country when new currenc, was introduced in 1932. A national bank had been established several years previously, and it became a favoured instrument of many of the shah's reforms. The transition from primarily silver coins to notes was a lengthy process in the development of finance, but payment in kind and barter, rather than payment in notes, continued long in the country and even today some nomads will refuse to deal with paper money. Naturally, a certain amount of inflation took place in Iran as elsewhere and, as usual, the common folk suffered the most. Iran had been set on the road to a modern economy by Reza Shah and she suffered all the pains of learning, frequently the hard way, that Westernization exacted a price for all of its benefits.

The ultimate source of change and growth in Iran was the political and legal authority, and under Reza Shah the pretense of elections, a parliament, and even briefly in early days political groupings rather than parties, was maintained. The *majlis*, the popular instrument of the implementation of the Constitution, as we have mentioned, now holds a special position in the loyalties of Persians. The representatives were and are anything but responsible to their constituents, the mass of people, yet the *majlis* was the only body in the government which seemed to listen to the public and in some measure was the voice of the people. In a very short time after 1906 the *majlis* became the symbol of the national will. Members of the *majlis* were usually resident in Tehran although all parts of the country were to be represented. Elections to the *majlis* were usually a farce, and many of the men were elected without opposition. In spite of this the forms of parliamentary government were established and a tradition came into being. Under Reza Shah elections were held and the *majlis* passed the laws, which the government of Reza Shah proposed. But the formalities of passing laws were observed and the structure of representative government was maintained even though the parliament was a rubber stamp for the shah's wishes.

Political parties had never existed in Iran but there had been both a liberal and a conservative group in parliament before World War I. After the chaos of the war the Communist party appeared on the scene. It had started among Iranian workers in the Baku oil fields in 1917. The Soviet occupation of Gilan gave a boost to the activities of the party in Iran and local cells flourished in the major cities. Other incipient parties did come into being during and after World War I. Under Reza Shah all political parties were abolished and the Communist party went underground working especially among minorities. Only after the abdication of Reza Shah did parties reappear, the most prominent one the Communist party called the *Tudeh* or 'masses' party.

The ideas of political democracy and the ballot were not well understood, to put it mildly, in Iran. This is best illustrated by a story widely spread, at least among foreign circles in Iran in the time of Reza Shah. A group of students were assembled and sent in a body to a polling place where they were given folded ballots to put in the boxes. When one of the students started to unfold his ballot before placing it in the box as directed, a policeman forbade him, and admonished him saying, 'Don't you know these are secret ballots?'

The foreign relations of Iran during Reza Shah's reign can be characterized as a decline of Soviet and British influences with a corresponding growth of German prestige. German technicians and teachers came in numbers to Iran. German architects designed many government buildings and most of the machinery for factories was German. By 1940 almost half of Iran's foreign trade was with Germany. The Junkers airline opened air service from Berlin to Tehran in 1937 and tourists came, some remaining in Iran. Propaganda from Irano-German cultural associations was strong, and the German effort to win Persian friendship was generally successful. While the Soviet Union and especially Great Britain tried to counteract the German propaganda they were not successful. The United States was too far away, and after the shah closed the mission schools, there was even less American influence in the country.

With the outbreak of World War II Iran held to the same position as the United States, and for both countries hostilities were far away. Nonetheless plans for continued expansion of Iran's economy had to be curtailed since Nazi Germany needed to concentrate its resources for the war in Europe. The German invasion of the Soviet Union changed the picture and with the rapid advance of Nazi forces in south Russia the Persians thought and hoped that their traditional foes to the north might be eliminated. The British and Russians, however, had plans for Iran. In July and August they sent notes to the Iranian government requesting the expulsion of several hundred Germans from the country. Reza Shah hesitated and since the two great powers received no satisfactory reply they invaded Iran on August 25, 1941.

Persian resistance collapsed completely after a few shots had been fired, and the façade of Reza Shah's army and his power collapsed as well. Reza Shah abdicated on September 16, 1941 and was succeeded by his young son, Mohammed Reza Pahlavi, but real power in the country was assumed by the two great powers the Russians in the north and the British in the south. The end of an era had come, and not until long after the war was Iran able to regain some measure of stability which had been lost with the passing of Reza Shah.

In retrospect it is difficult to assess the achievements of Reza Shah. We must remember that the cataclysm of World War I which dealt a death blow to the old order of things in Europe, also prepared the way for Reza Shah in Iran. The deterministic school of history would have one believe that the times produced the man to deal with the crisis at hand, and that the appearance of a person such as Reza Shah was inevitable and necessary. There is no question that Reza Shah gave Iran a shock treatment and changed the face of the land. Iranians who decry the backwardness of their country should remember how it was in the not too distant past before Reza Shah. If they further complain that parts of their country are still as they always were, medieval and virtually untouched by the modern world, then they should not overlook the areas of backwardness which exist in almost every country of the globe.

Reza Shah turned Iran upside down and even though the comic-opera nature of some of his reforms, such as the construction of an opera house in Tehran, cannot be denied, yet the very shaking of Iran which he did was epochal in character. The stories told about his foibles, and the terror which the old shah inspired, are legion, and he will go down in history as the Rustam of his age, the new hero of story tellers. Not since Shah 'Abbas have the *raconteurs* had such a fine subject, even greater than Nadir Shah or any of the Qajars. One may criticize Reza Shah in many ways but his greatness cannot be denied and his shadow rests heavily on the future of Iran.

CHAPTER IX

The New Iran

IF the following lines had been written a decade or more ago it might have been entitled 'changes which do not change'. For, in spite of such spectacular developments as the nationalization of the Anglo-Iranian Oil Company in 1951 and its aftermath, one would have had a difficult task to show fundamental changes in the economy or the society of Iran. But in recent years change has occurred, fundamental change not only in the outward manifestations of a remarkable growth in many areas, but more significantly change in outlook and belief among various sections of the population. Even peasants now are clamouring for more reforms and more of the fruits of an expanding economy, which a country with limited natural resources like Iran may find difficult to provide in the future. The concentration of power in the hands of the ruler and the growth in influence of the military may cloud the future, but at the end of the decade of the 1960s Iran has reached a plateau of prosperity and stability which will give time for the changes to become integrated into new institutions, or new social organizations.

It would be difficult to give a date to the change, for example, in the attitude of many Persians towards capital investment. Only one who had lived in Iran through the period from World War II to the present could appreciate the change in the psychology of the businessmen, or in the atmosphere in which this happened. In that era hardly one Persian business-man was willing to gamble on the re-investment of his profits in expansion of activities or plant, preferring instead to send money to Swiss banks or elsewhere abroad. Likewise, many Persians felt that only foreigners would or could develop their country, for trust and confidence in their fellowmen were largely lacking. Today banks proliferate and Persian money has returned from abroad. It is true that with the rapid growth of industry and business and speculation in Iran, profits have been far larger at home than abroad, but more important for many, stability and growth seem assured for the future. The country no longer requires foreign aid, and Persian entrepreneurs are developing their own country.

This last is vital, for Iran is moving well and fast under its own power, and this has changed the general outlook so much that one can speak of a new Iran in the latter part of the twentieth century. Perhaps one should accept the contention of the government of Iran that the 'White Revolution' from above, which was approved by a massive referendum vote of the people on January 26, 1963, marked the beginning of a revolution. In that referendum Shah Mohammed Reza Pahlavi proposed five basic reforms, approval of the Land Reform Act which abolished the serf-landlord establishment, the nationalization of all forests, the sale of government-owned factories to act as surety for land reforms, the allotment of a share of the net profits of factories to the workers, amendments to the Election Law including women's suffrage, and finally the formation of a Literacy Corps to help implement the goal of compulsory universal education. These proved not to be empty words, as so often in the past, but bills were passed in the *majlis* to implement the programme and progress is being made.

Some three-quarters of the population of Iran is engaged in agriculture, so land reform is very important to the life of the country. The shah began to distribute crown and state lands as early as 1951, but the great landowners did not follow suit. Consequently, according to new laws, a landowner was permitted to retain only one village in his possession where previously a few landowners had owned hundreds of villages, as well as land amounting almost to a small province. The landowners were required to sell their excess land to the state, which then resold them to farmers who were to pay for their newly acquired land in annual instalments over a fifteen year period. The Agriculture Bank was the organ for the transfer of land. Minimum land holdings were instituted, but rural and farm co-operatives were encouraged. The idea spread and today there are over 5,000 co-operatives in the country.

The landlords were repaid in great part by shares in government owned factories, which were thus turned over to private ownership as part of the 'White Revolution'. The meshing of various parts of the programme was not only ingenious but, more important in the Iranian context, it worked. The prestige, ability, and drive of the shah had moved the country in a manner unprecedented. By so doing he had aroused opposition on all sides, and yet he had triumphed in that the vast majority of the common people not only approved but enthusiastically followed him. The liberals and leftists, including remnants of the Tudeh or 'masses' party, the Communist party of Iran after World War II but long banned, found their thunder taken from them by a shah who imposed daring reforms far beyond the expectations of many liberals. The landowners and old aristocracy were not happy at their loss of privilege and power, and finally the religious leaders were aroused by the shah's emancipation of women and other reforms considered to be anti-Islamic in spirit.

To return to the reforms, the nationalization of forests seems to be a relatively small measure in comparison with the others, but in a land like Iran where trees are such a blessing in comparison with the arid and stony landscape the protection of trees is almost a sacred duty. Together with the nationalization of forest land went measures to protect the land from goats, and large projects of afforestation to be launched over a period of years. Rows of saplings have been planted near Tehran and provincial centres, and bureaus for the implementation of measures designed to protect trees have been established.

Up until 1953, when the post-war era of intense nationalism ended with the overthrow of Dr Mohammed Mossadegh, the prime minister who engineered the nationalization of the Anglo-Iranian Oil Company, and led a combine of rabid nationalists in a political grouping called the National Front, the government owned and operated the overwhelming majority of industries in Iran. This was a legacy from the inter-war period of Reza Shah when state control threatened to monopolize ownership of all industries. The few private enterprises were mainly in the textile industry, whereas sugar, cement, matches, and other basic industries were almost wholly state owned. Since 1953 the government has encouraged private enterprise in industry through concession and special facilities granted to investors such as customs and tax exemptions, aid in exports and the like. In ten years, from 1953, the number of factories in the country, excluding the enormous oil industry, fisheries, railroads and tobacco plants, rose from 1,300 to 10,247, while the number of workers went up from 7,500 to 139,000. For other increases see the appendix.

The government enacted many laws pertaining to the working conditions of workers, including the sharing of profits between employers and employees. It is impossible to discuss the many measures which have given social security, health insurance and other benefits to labourers. The Workers' Welfare Bank has led the way in educating the workers in how to save for future housing, and many other activities. Again, the contrast with the bazaar money changers and loan sharks who ruled finance only a few years ago, is overwhelming.

The Literacy Corps (*sipah-ye danesh*) has been a most successful project, which gives university graduates subject to military service the option of serving in the countryside to help the villagers. The educated young men from the cities not only teach the villagers, old and young, to read and write, but they also aid them with sanitation, health problems and construction. So successful was the Literacy Corps that a Health Corps on similar lines was proclaimed by the ruler in January 1964. One could continue with developments in the judiciary, in commerce, roads and communications, but the story would be the same, great expansion and new developments which are still changing the country.

The change is there for all to see. Not only has there been an overall increase in the amount of land under cultivation and of general harvests, but the yield per acre has increased almost everywhere on land which has received benefits from the revolution. The railroad has been extended to Meshed in the east and to Tabriz in the north from Tehran. If one had said a generation ago that Persian rail lines would someday reach the Turkish line in the west and Pakistan in the east, no one would have taken him seriously. Today anything seems possible. Two and one half days were formerly required to reach Shiraz from Tehran over miserable roads. Today fleets of buses make the journey in one day. Coca-cola competes with Pepsi-cola in the most isolated villages, and so it goes.

Material progress is enormous but much remains to be done, for large parts of Iran in the mountains and deserts are just emerging from the Middle Ages, and the jet age of the capital is still far from many villagers and nomads. In a sense the task has only begun, but it has begun and begun well, which is important. Iran has come far from the dark days of World War II when the country was occupied by the Allies. How did Iran come of age?

When British and Russian forces moved into Iran in the autumn of 1941, Reza Shah abdicated and the fate of the monarchy was in jeopardy. But the Allies agreed to the succession of the son of Reza Shah, the present ruler. Iran became a bridge of supplies sent to the Soviet Union and thus contributed to the Allied victory. During the war the people suffered from a lack of supplies, an enormous inflation, and even hunger. On the other hand, many Persians learned about automobiles, organization of supplies and transport from Soviet, British and American troops who occupied the country. There was also a revival of political activity; groups formed about leading personalities, and one desciplined and organized party came to the fore, the Tudeh or Communist party. In spite of the physical difficulties of life, Iran in the war period was shaken out of a kind of complacency which had rested on the will and personality of one man, Reza Shah. Iran would never return to what it had been before Reza Shah, but for a long time his shadow remained over various Persian leaders groping for a road to the future.

It would take too many pages to detail the important events in the history of Iran from 1945 to 1953, a period which might be characterized as one of intense nationalisms, frequently opposed to one another or going in opposite directions. All were searching for a programme or a philosophy to lead the country out of the uncertainties of the post-war period to stability yet progress. For a time it seemed, however, as though in political matters Iran would return to the Qajar age when politicians were tools of Russia or Britain, only now with the U.S.A. assuming more and more the role of the British. Although in the case of the Tudeh party and various conservative groups, history seemed to repeat itself, new movements such as the rightist Sumka and Iranvej parties, if one can use the word party for those associations, complicated the picture. One common feature united all of them, and that was an intense patriotism and nationalistic fervour.

The power of the new nationalism was revealed, I believe, as early as 1946, when both the Azerbaijan Democrat government in Tabriz, and the Kurdish republic in Mahabad failed to rally support against the central government after Soviet troops were withdrawn from northern Iran. Many people failed to understand that particular quality of Iranian society which had developed over the centuries, and which gave a sense of identity to the nation, based on the Persian language, on a Persian culture, and on a Persian religion. For, as nowhere else in the Middle East, Iran had a strong sense of its difference from the rest of the Islamic world, and Azerbaijan was part of that cultural complex, even though the people spoke Turkish. The issue was not whether Azerbaijan belonged to Iran or not, because few doubted that it did, and those who thought they could separate the northwest part of the country from the rest were really out of date. Furthermore, the relation of the Azerbaijanis to other Iranians, has been somewhat similar to the Scots who claimed, perhaps rightly, that they ran the British Empire. The important issue at stake in the post-war period until 1953 was rather who was going to run the entire country, or at least influence its future, among the various groups of nationalists with different theories.

It is an interesting commentary on Iranian history that whereas under the Qajars the religious elements were in the ascendancy *vis-à-vis* the political establishment, the roles were reversed in the post World War II period, and much of this was the result of the success of Reza Shah in reasserting the supremacy of the secular ruling institution. The Qajars had been weak, defeated by Russia and highly regarded by few. The religious leaders had usurped the position of prestige and power, as shown by their influence in the Constitutionalist movement, but after Reza Shah religious leaders were divided among themselves, and gave their allegiances to one or another of the nationalist groups who now had the initiative. Almost everyone paid lip service to the official religion of the state, but almost as a matter of course, for the religious establishment no longer mattered. Furthermore, since Shiism in Iran had been so long identified with the state, there was no tradition in it of opposition to the state. Any opposition had to be expressed in personal terms, or as terrorism against individuals.

The culmination of the constant conflict and competition of rival nationalist groups both inside and outside of the Majlis was the emotion charged régime of Dr Mohammed

Mossadegh. He became prime minister, after the assassination of his predecessor General Razmara, who had counselled moderation in dealing with the oil problem, on April 29, 1951 the day a law was passed nationalizing the Anglo-Iranian Oil Company. The British government failed to appreciate the intensity of feeling, and the symbolic nature of the nationalization of oil in the overall nationalist agitation of the day. A universal tide of sentiment united the vast majority of Persians in their desire to remove foreign control of their greatest industry and natural resource. Subsequent events provided world newspapers with ample copy for many months. The great petroleum companies of the world boycotted the oil of Iran and the Persians could not market their oil. The economic situation in Iran grew desperate and the United Nations also wrestled with the oil problem. Inside Iran, but especially in the capital, street mobs intimidated the government. For example, on July 16, 1952 when Dr Mossadegh resigned as prime minister because of strong opposition in the parliament, Ahmad Ghavam his successor lasted only four days because of the street riots and fighting against the police and security forces. The street demonstrations had influenced a change in government and followers of the National Front, as well as the Tudeh party, were quick to realize new possibilities of influence.

Dr Mossadegh again became premier. He had assumed mistakenly that Great Britain could not survive without Iranian oil, but Saudi Arabia, Kuwait and Iraq increased their oil production to replace Persian oil, a situation to be repeated in reverse, by Iran, during the Arab-Israeli war of the summer of 1967. No progress resulted from proposals to settle the oil dispute, so on October 22, 1952 Iran broke diplomatic relations with Great Britain. Thus another chapter in Iran's recent history saw the end of the British position as the most influential foreign interest in the country in modern times. Neither the United States nor any other country was to assume the role which the British had played for so many years in the country.

The failure of the Mossadegh government to solve the oil crisis, and the threatened economic collapse of the country incited opposition to the prime minister. Dr Mossadegh responded with arrests and martial law. One of the supporters of Mossadegh who then became an opponent was a prominent religious leader Abu'l-Qassem Kashani, who was almost a spiritual leader of extremist religious fanatics. The opposition of the upper house of the legislature, the Senate which had come into existence only after Word War II, and of the shah, convinced Mossadegh he would have to limit their powers. He dissolved the Senate and proposed measures to limit the power of the ruler. The lower house of *majlis* could not be controlled as easily as the Senate, so a referendum was held which voted power to Mossadegh also to dissolve the *majlis*, which he did at the beginning of August 1953. Thus Mossadegh openly flaunted and side-stepped the royal decree needed to formalize the dissolution of the *majlis*. The ruler fought back, issuing a decree dismissing Mossadegh as prime minister and appointing a retired general, Zahedi as premier. Mossadegh refused to obey and arrested the commander of the royal guard who brought him the order. At this news the shah, who was staying in Mazanderan, left the country by flying to Rome.

The departure of Mohammed Reza Shah on August 16, 1953 was a signal for the Tudeh party to move. A democratic republic was proclaimed by Communist agents who organized street demonstrations. Dr Mossadegh, who had remained in his home in Tehran in his familiar pajamas for many weeks, was powerless to prevent the disorders and riots. On August 19th, General Zahedi led army units into Tehran, and after brief fighting arrested Dr Mossadegh and suppressed the Tudeh led riots. During those three days of demonstrations statues of the shah and his father had been pulled down by demonstrators and it seemed as though the monarchy had come to an end. The experiences of August 1953 made the shah resolve

H

that he, rather than the fickle parliament, would lead the country. This he has done since 1953.

The year following the overthrow of Dr Mossadegh was spent in preparing for new elections to the Senate and *majlis* which took place in February 1964. Much legislation of the Mossadegh period had to be repealed or revised, and an oil agreement was needed to start revenues flowing again into the empty coffers of the government. In October an agreement was ratified by both houses of parliament which created a consortium composed of representatives of eight international petroleum companies to market the oil of Iran. The new oil agreement was not all that Iran desired, but it provided for stability, compensation for the old Anglo-Iranian Oil Company, and a recognition of Iran's ownership of all oil facilities and resources in the country.

The army was purged of Tudeh agents and credits were obtained from Great Britain and the U.S.A. to help the bad fiscal condition of the Persian government. Further, in the spring of 1955 an agreement was concluded between the U.S.S.R. and Iran which liquidated the debts and financial claims of the two countries incurred during World War II. The stage was cleared for a programme of reform and development.

At this time perhaps the most important instrument of economic reform was the second Seven Year Plan, the first having died before weaning in the hectic days of Dr Mossadegh. Oil revenues as well as foreign credits were allocated to the Plan Organization, and although many of the goals of the Plan were not achieved, the nation was given a blueprint for development which laid the basis for the more recent expansion.

It is unnecessary to follow the changes in cabinets, and the elections since 1960 when the government of Dr Manuchehr Eghbal resigned after lasting over three years, almost a record. A certain political stability was reached when on March 7, 1964 the leader of a new party called 'Modern Iran', Hasan

Ali Mansur, was appointed prime minister. The parliament with which Mansur had to deal was also quite different from previous parliaments, for a number of women and workers and peasants had been elected to the *majlis*, formerly almost the exclusive prerogative of the landlords. Unfortunately on January 21, 1965 Mansur was shot at the entrance to the *majlis* and died shortly afterwards.

The Minister of Finances in Mansur's cabinet, Amir Abbas Hoveyda, was appointed prime minister, and he continued Mansur's policies. It was primarily under the régimes of Mansur and Hoveyda that the changes outlined above began to bear fruit, and the process continues at an accelerated pace.

Political assassinations have been mentioned several times, and they have played a role in the modern history of Iran. Assassination is an old tradition of religious fanaticism in Iran, and it has devotees even today, although the religious establishment is weaker today than at any time since early Safavid times. Since the religious-state controversy may prove to be the most important problem of the future of Iran, we should examine it from an overall point of view.

In a certain sense the Asiatic country which best presents a parallel to Iran throughout her history is Japan. Both countries were early conscious of their differences from their neighbours, which gave birth to a sense of national identity earlier than elsewhere. In Japan the Shinto religion became identified as the Japanese state religion, with both state and religion presided over by the emporer. In Sasanian Iran Zoroastrianism was the state religion and both state and religion were presided over by the king of kings. From Safavid times to the present the state religion has been Shiite Islam of the twelve Imams, and the ruler was the acknowledged head of the church-state complex. In the Sasanian and Safavid empires the position of the ruler weakened towards the end of both dynasties, but the religious establishments in both cases were not powerful enough to take the place of the ruler. Iran like Japan, had a 'nationalist' religion which was not universal. In times of political crises, and especially in the formation of dynasties, a 'national' religion could be of great aid to the political power, a rallying point for Iranians, but such a religion, bound as it was, to one state, lacked ecumenical force or appeal. It is hard to imagine Shiite missionaries converting any non-Iranian Sunnis to their persuasion. Shiite Islam has been a great support for the political structure of one country, Iran, and therein lies its weakness. True, the religious leaders in the past have saved themselves by withdrawal in times of political turmoil, practicing the traditions of *taqiyeh* or *kitman,* 'dissimulation', but this has only enabled them to survive. One misses here the message to all mankind which is the glory of at least Sunni Islam and Christianity. The power of these last two to integrate diverse peoples and societies may seem a weakness when specific action is required, but one wonders about the fate of such as Shiite Islam and Shintoism in a modern world which is so interdependent and so ecumenical.

With all of the material progress in recent years, Iran at present can be divided into an educated élite plus a middle class concerned mostly with economic development and political power, and the masses of peasants and workers, who hold to Shiite Islam as their guide to social, political and economic, as well as religious problems. For the first group, Shiism is irrelevant; they have outgrown it, and regard it as little more than a support for nationalism, or as a national cult which is useful. The opposition which some of the intellectuals feel against it may be based ultimately on the feeling mentioned above that Iranian Shiism is too narrow, restricts their intellectual horizons, and isolates them from their neighbours and from the world. This irrelevance of their religion to the problem of national identity is not realized or understood by the masses, who still feel the need for, and power of, a national religion. The dilemma of the religious leaders lies in this division in Iranian society. The government and the educated no longer need the active support of the religious leaders, yet the religious leaders fear that they will lose their influence over the masses if they give up the connection with the state. Perhaps the religious leaders will turn more to religious matters which do concern multitudes, rather than seek to re-establish an outmoded relationship. In any case, Iran is in a state of transition and religion cannot maintain age old attitudes in the face of universal change.

The coronation of the shah in October 1967 was more than a glittering show which, among other things, presented to the world the once isolated and overgrown ruins of Persepolis as a prime tourist attraction. It marked the end of Iran's need for foreign aid and the coming of age of the country as the leading nation of the Middle East, perhaps now ready to play a role beyond its own frontiers. The strength, economic progress and independence of Iran may serve as a beacon to her neighbours, but unless the country can assume an intellectual and even spiritual leadership by breaking its past isolation and sense of uniqueness, no one will listen. The glorious traditions of the past need not weigh down Iran, but rather provide an impetus for a new material and spiritual synthesis for a glorious future. In the trying years ahead for all mankind the Persian people, one feels sure, will not only survive in the modern world, but will take their place in the common effort to promote the welfare of all mankind. *Iran zinde bad*, 'long live Iran'.

APPENDIX I

SELECTED FIGURES IN THE DEVELOPMENT OF IRAN*

	1953	1963
Refined sugar	60,000 tons	217,000 tons
Cotton cloth	60 million metres	418 million metres
Capacity of poultry incubators	5,000 chickens	20 million chickens
Power of telegraph transmitters	4 KW per day	41 KW per day
Oil production	c. 130 million barrels	580 million barrels
Capacity of ports of Khorramshahr and Bandar Shapur	870,000 tons	2,000,000 tons
Number of factories	1,300	10,247
Workers covered by social security	325,000 workers	1,550,000 workers
Number of students in primary schools	730,793	1,841,201
Number of students at college and higher educational institutes	8,918	24,885

*Taken from official Iranian government publications such as Ali Asghar Shamem, *Iran in the Reign of His Majesty Mohammad Reza Shah Pahlavi* (Tehran 1965); Ashraf Ahmadi, *Twelve Years in Constructing a new Iran* (Tehran, n.d.), and serial publications.

APPENDIX II

CHRONOLOGY OF IMPORTANT EVENTS

612 B.C.	Conquest of Nineveh by Medes
549	Victory of Cyrus over Medes
539	Conquest of Babylon by Cyrus
490	Battle of Marathon
330	Alexander conquers Iran
323	Death of Alexander
3rd to 1st century B.C.	Graeco-Bactrian kingdom
312 B.C.	Seleucus enters Babylon, beginning of Seleucid era
141	Mithradates of Parthia enters Seleucia
53 B.C.	Parthians annihilate Roman army at Carrhae
226 A.D.	Ardashir and Sasanian Dynasty replace Parthians
531 A.D.	Chosroes Anosharvan becomes ruler
637	Arabs destroy Sasanian army at Qadisiyah
661-750	Umayyad Caliphate rules over Iran
750-1055	Iran part of 'Abbasid Caliphate
999	Ferdosi finishes his 'Book of Kings'
1055	Seljuk Turks capture Baghdad
1219	Beginning of Mongol conquest of Iran
1380	Timur commences conquest of Iran
1405	Death of Timur
1502	Ismail Safavi occupies Tabriz and starts Safavid Dynasty
1514	Defeat of Safavids by Ottomans at Chaldiran
1587	Shah 'Abbas moves capital to Isfahan
1722	Capture of Isfahan by Afghans and fall of the Safavids
1736	Nadir Shah embarks on conquests
1747	Nadir Shah assassinated
1794	Aga Muhammad establishes Qajar dynasty

1797	Fath Ali Shah ascends throne
1813	Gulistan peace treaty between Russia and Iran
1828	Turkomanchai treaty between Russia and Iran
1850	Bab executed
1857	Persians evacuate Herat after war with England
1901	D'Arcy oil concession in Iran signed
1906	(December 30th) Constitution proclaimed
1907	Anglo-Russian Agreement dividing Iran into zones of influence
1908-1909	Persian Revolution
1911	(December) Russian and British Troops occupy zones
1918	Beginning of revolution in Gilan
1921	(February 26th) Soviet-Iranian treaty signed
1923	Reza Khan becomes Prime Minister
1925	(December 12th) Reza Shah crowned; establishes Pahlavi dynasty
1928	National Bank of Iran founded
1933	Anglo-Persian Oil agreement revised
1938	Trans-Iranian RR finished
1941	(August 25th) Soviet and British troops occupy Iran
1945	Azerbaijan and Kurdish governments formed
1946	(December) Fall of two governments above
1951-1953	Dr Mossadegh and the nationalization of oil

APPENDIX III

THE NATIONAL DYNASTIES OF IRAN

I. Achaemenids

Cyrus	559-530 B.C.
Cambyses	530-522
Darius	522-486
Xerxes	486-465
Artaxerxes I	465-424
Xerxes II	424-423
Darius II	423-404
Artaxerxes II	404-359
Artaxerxes III	359-338
Arses	338-336
Darius III	336-330

II. Parthians (early rulers not noted)

Mithradates I	c. 171-138 B.C.
Phraates II	c. 138-128
Artabanus II	c. 128-123
Mithradates II	c. 123-87
Gotarzes I	c. 91-80
Orodes	c. 80-76
Sinatruces	c. 76-70
Phraates III	c. 70-57
Mithradates III	c. 57-55
Orodes II	c. 57-37
Phraates IV	c. 37-2
Tiridates II	c. 30-25
Phraataces	c. 2 B.C.-4 A.D.
Orodes III	c. 4-7 A.D.
Vonones I	c. 7-12
Artabanus III	c. 12-38

Tiridates III	c. 36
Vardanes	c. 39-47
Gotarzes II	c. 38-51
Vonones II	c. 51
Vologeses I	c. 51-80
Pacorus	c. 79-115
Oroses	c. 109-128
Artabanus IV	c. 80-81
Vologeses II	c. 105-147
Mithradates IV	c. 128-147
Vologeses III	c. 148-192
Vologeses IV	c. 191-207
Vologeses V	c. 207-227
Artabanus V	c. 213-224
Artavasdes	c. 226-227

III. Sasanians

Ardashir	c. 224-240
Shapur I	c. 240-272
Hormizd Ardashir	c. 272-273
Bahram I	c. 273-276
Bahram II	276-293
Bahram III	293
Nerseh	293-302
Hormizd II	302-309
Shapur II	309-379
Ardashir II	379-383
Shapur III	383-388
Bahram IV	388-399
Yazdegird I	399-421
Bahram V	421-439
Yazdegird II	439-457
Hormizd III	457-459
Peroz	459-484
Valash	484-488
Kavad	488-531
Zamasp	496-498
Chosroes I	531-579
Hormizd IV	579-590
Chosroes II	591-628

Kavad II	628
Ardashir III	628-629
Boran	629-630
Hormizd V, Chosroes III	630-632
Yazdegird III	632-651

IV. Safavids

Shah Ismail	1502-1524
Tahmasp I	1524-1576
Ismail II	1576-1577
Mohammed Khudabanda	1578-1587
Shah 'Abbas I	1587-1629
Safi I	1629-1641
'Abbas II	1642-1667
Sulayman	1667-1694
Husain	1694-1722
Tahmasp II	1722-1732
'Abbas III	1732-1736
Nadir Shah	1736-1747
Karim Khan Zand	1750-1779

V. Qajars

Aga Mohammed	1794-1797
Fath 'Ali	1797-1835
Mohammed	1835-1848
Nasr ad-Din	1848-1896
Muzaffer ad-Din	1896-1906
Mohammed 'Ali	1907-1909
Ahmad	1909-1925

VI. Pahlavi

Reza Shah	1925-1941
Mohammed Arya Mehr	1941-

BIBLIOGRAPHY

Rather than merely list titles of various books, I have decided to mention works in categories not usually found in bibliographies. The reader may find this method unorthodox but perhaps some will welcome a change from standard bibliographies, several of which exist such as L. P. Elwell-Sutton, *Guide to Iranian Area Study* (Washington, D.C., 1952); G. M. Wickens and R. Savory, *Persia in Islamic Times* (McGill University, Montreal 1964). Iran is included in the *Index Islamicus* (Cambridge, 1962) edited by J. D. Pearson.

A. Fictional satires on society and government:

1. James Morier, *Hajji Baba of Isfahan,* first published in London 1823, this classic about life under the early Qajars gives a good picture of the common people and their foibles.
2. Karguiz Effendi (pseudonym for Jacques de Morgan), *Le Chah de Mahboulistan* (Paris, 1913), gives a fictional account of the court at the end of the Qajar period.
3. Richard Waughburton (pseudonym for Robert Byron and Christopher Sykes), *Innocence and Design* (Macmillan, London, 1936), is a satire on the reign of Reza Shah.
4. Leo Vaughn, *The Jokeman* (Eyre and Spotswood, London, 1961). The last half of the book describes the life of a foreign teacher in southern Persia.

B. Travels and life in Persia:

1. E. G. Browne, *A Year Amongst the Persians* (Black, London, 1950). A scholarly account of ordinary life in old Iran.
2. G. Bell, *Persian Pictures* (London, 1947), is excellent writing about Persia before World War I.
3. Olive Suratgar, *I Sing in the Wilderness* (London, 1951). An English woman married to a Persian gives insight into social affairs.
4. Anne Sinclair Mehdevi, *Persian Adventure* (New York, 1953). An American married to a Persian delightfully describes family life of post World War II Iran.

C. Novels of Persians:

1. B. Y. Mirza, *Stripling* (New York, 1940) is an interesting account of a Persian youth growing up.

2. Sadegh Hedayat, *The Blind Owl* (New York, 1958), describes the psychological sufferings of Persian intellectuals.

3. Fereidoun Isfandiary, *The Day of Sacrifice* (London, 1960), and other novels by the same author depict the problems of Persians in a changing world.

D. Histories of Iran:

1. R. N. Frye, *The Heritage of Persia* (London, 1963) is a short account of pre-Islamic Iran with an extensive bibliography.

2. J. Rypka, *A History of Iranian Literature* (Leiden, 1967) is an encyclopedia of the literature of Iran from earliest times to the present with an extensive bibliography.

3. B. Spuler, *Iran in Früh-Islamischer Zeit* (Wiesbaden, 1952), and his *Die Mongolen in Iran* 1220-1350 (Wiesbaden, 1965) are two full works on Iran after the Arab conquests.

4. L. L. Bellan, *Chah Abbas I* (Paris, 1932) is the only biography of the great Safavid ruler in a Western language.

5. L. Lockhart. *The Fall of the Safavid Dynasty and The Afghan Occupation of Persia* (Cambridge 1958) and his *Nadir Shah* (London 1938) are the only general books on this period in a Western language.

6. E. G. Browne, *The Persian Revolution of* 1905-1909 (Cambridge 1910) is a classic about the revolution, written at that time.

7. P. Avery, *Modern Iran* (London 1965) is the best account of recent history in English.

8. R. Cottam, *Nationalism in Iran* (Pittsburgh 1964) gives a sympathetic account of the Mossadegh regime.

9. R. Ramazani, *The Foreign Policy of Iran,* 1500-1941 (University of Virginia Press, Charlottesville 1961), and S. Zabih, *The Communist Movement in Iran* (University of California Press 1967) deal with special subjects, while the autobiographical book by the present Shah, *Mission for my Country* (London), is a justification for his policies of recent years.

INDEX

Abadan, 15
'Abbas, Shah, 32-33, 63, 74-75, 88
'Abbas Mirza, 79
'Abbasid, 30, 32, 57
Achaemenids, 13, 16, 19, 21, 23, 25-27, 29, 36-38, 41-42, 44, 56, 66, 68
Afghan, 13, 66, 73-74, 77, 79
Aga Khan, 58
Aga Muhammad, 75
Ahmad Shah, 86, 90
Ahriman, 53
Ahura Mazda, 53
Alexander the Great, 27, 29, 37
'Ali, 30, 50, 58
'Ali Muhammad, Bab, 80
American, 18, 23, 42, 82, 88, 110
Anatolia, 31
Anglican missionaries, 82
Anglo-Persian Oil Co., 98, 105, 112, 114
Antiochus of Commagene, 29
Arab, 15-16, 18-19, 21, 23-24, 30-31, 34, 39-40, 65
Arabi Pasha, 83
Arabia, 20
Aramaic, 27
Ardashir Papakan, 30
Aristotle, 65
Armenia(n), 24, 40, 69, 76, 78, 83, 88, 97
Arsaces, 28
Aryan, 13, 24, 53, 58
'asabiyyah, 18, 35, 71
Assassins, 58
Assyria(n), 25-26, 36-37, 82-83
Avesta, 45, 53
Ayatullah Burujirdi, 61
Azerbaijan, 14, 17, 24, 31, 84, 111
Azerbaijan Democrat, 110
Azeris, 17, 80, 84

Babism, 64, 80-81
Babur, 32
Babylonia, 19, 25-26
Baha'ullah, 81
Bahaism, 20, 55, 64, 83, 97
Bahrain, 77
Bakhtiyaris, 16
Baku, 77, 84, 101
Baluchis, 13, 15-16, 24, 98
Bandar 'Abbas, 75
Begram, 37
Behdukht, 59

Behistun, 44
Behzad, 40
Bibi Shahrbanu, 45
Bolshevik, 87
Brahui, 24
British, 75-76, 78-79, 81-83, 85, 87, 98, 102-103, 109, 114
British Museum, 37
Buddhist, 37
Burushaski, 24
Byzantine, 26

Carmelites, 76
Caspian Sea, 15, 76, 92
Caucasus, 13
Central Asia, 23, 31, 38, 76, 89
China, 38, 42
Chinese, 21
Chinggis Khan, 31-32
Christian, 19, 57, 62, 69, 77, 116
Circassian, 63
Communist, 18, 42, 101, 107, 113
Ctesias, 28
Cyrus, 28

Darius, 25-26, 41, 44
Dasht-i Kavir, 13
Dasht-i Lut, 13
Davar, 94
Delhi, 73
Derbend, 77
dihqan, 67
Dutch East India Co., 75

East India Co., 75
Eghbal, Manuchehr, 114
Egypt, 19, 25-26, 36, 39, 78
Elamites, 25
Elburz, 14-15
England, 34
English (see British), 18, 75, 88

Farmanfarmaian, 26
Fars, 14, 17
Fath 'Ali Shah, 45, 79-80, 82
Fedayan-i Islam, 58
Firdosi, 18, 30, 34, 45
France, 17, 23, 34, 50, 82, 97
French, 18, 31, 76, 78-79, 97, 103

Gathas, 53
Georgian, 63, 77-78, 88
German(y), 17, 21, 31, 85, 87, 98, 102
Ghavam, 112

Ghazzali, 65
Gilan, 15, 77, 87, 91
Golden Horde, 31
Goths, 38
Greek, 13, 26-29, 36, 38, 54
Gulistan, 43

Hafez, 18, 46
Haidar, 32
Haifa, 81
Hatra, 37
Herat, 13, 40
Herodotus, 19, 21, 26, 28
Hormuz, 75
Hoveyda, Amir Abbas, 115
Hungary, 38
Hunza, 24
Husain, 58
Hydarnes, 22

Ibn Khaldun, 18, 64
imamzadeh, 59
India, 23, 42, 49-50, 58, 64, 76, 83
Indo-European, 23-25
Iranvej party, 110
Iraq, 13, 16, 112
Isfahan, 40, 71-73, 75-77, 86
Isfandiyar, 30
Ishraqi, 65
Islam, 23, 30-31, 39, 55-59, 67
Ismail, Shaikh, 32, 63
Ismailis, 58
Israel, 112
Istanbul, 63

Jalal al-Din Rumi, 46
Jamal al-Din Afghani, 83
Janissaries, 63
Japan, 43, 50, 85, 115
Jesuits, 76
Jews, 19, 25, 54, 57, 69, 83
Junkers airline, 102
Justin, 28

Karen, 41
Karim Khan Zand, 74
Kashan, 71
Kashani, Abu'l-Qassem, 113
Kaveh, 31
Kazem Reshti, 80
Kemal Ataturk, 34, 89
Kerbela, 16
Khaksariyya, 59
Khorsabad, 37
Khurasan, 13, 17, 30, 59
Khuzistan, 15-16, 91
Kirman, 17, 59, 71, 99
Koh-i Taftan, 15
Kurdistan, 25, 91, 98, 110

Kurds, 13, 16, 29, 38, 59, 66
Kuwait, 112

Lenin, 18
Levantine, 69-70, 82
Louis XIV, 76
Luristan, 38
Lurs, 16, 24, 38
Lutfullah, Shaikh, 40

Mahabad, 110
majlis, 34, 87-88, 95, 101, 106, 113-115
Manichaeism, 20, 54-55
Mannaeans, 25
Mansur, Hasan Ali, 115
Manzanderan, 15, 77, 92, 99, 113
Marxist, 47
Mashhad, 59, 82, 87, 92, 100
Mazdak, 48, 54, 81
Medes, 25-26
Merovingian, 38
Mesopotamia (see Iraq), 16, 20, 25, 37
Millspaugh, 93
Mir Damad, 64
Mirza Taqi Khan, 80
Mithradates of Pontus, 29
Moghul, 32, 49, 64
Mohammed Reza Pahlavi, 35, 103, 106
Mongol, 31-32, 38, 63, 68-69
Morier, James, 43, 67
Moses, 28, 80
Mossadegh, Dr., 51, 108, 112-114
Muhammad, 16, 30, 32, 80, 88
Muhammad al-'Amili, 64
Muhammad 'Ali Shah, 85-86
Muhammad Baqir-i Majlisi, 64
mujtahid, 60-61, 64, 96
mullah, 60-62, 85
Mulla Sadra, 64-65
Muslim, 19
Mussolini, 89
Mu'tazilite, 57
Muzaffar al-Din, 84

Nadir Shah, 73-74, 77, 104
Napoleon, 78
Nasr al-Din Shah, 59, 80, 83
Nasir al-Din Tusi, 65
Nazi, 102
Nejef, 16, 80
Nimatallah Vali, 59
Nimrud Dagh, 29

Omar Khayyam, 46
Ossetes, 13
Ottoman, 49-50, 63, 65, 69, 76-78, 81-83, 88

Pahlavi, 46
Pakistan, 58, 109
Palestine, 25
Pan-Iranian, 13
Parthian, 16, 29, 36-38, 45, 54
Pasargadai, 25
Péguy, 23
Persepolis, 37, 117
Persis, 13
Peter the Great, 76-77, 90
Pompey, 29
Portuguese, 75
Presbyterian missionaries, 82
Protestant, 57, 82

Qajar, 26, 32–34, 40–41, 45, 49, 51, 55, 67–68, 75, 79, 88, 91, 94, 104
Qashgai, 17, 87, 96
Qavam al-Sultaneh, 66
Qizilbash, 33, 63
Qum, 59–61, 71, 96
Qur'an, 57, 80, 94, 97

Rawalpindi, 42
Razmara, 112
Resht, 77, 82, 86
Reuter, Baron de, 83
Reza Shah, 16, 29, 34, 40–41, 50–51, 67–68, 70–71, 74, 77, 79, 88–104, 110–111
Rezaiyeh, 82
Rhazes, 71
Roman, 29, 73
Roman Catholic, 57, 75, 82
Romulus and Remus, 28
Russia, 31, 48, 50–51, 76–79, 81–82, 85–87, 98
Rustam, 30, 104

Sa'di, 18, 41, 43
Safavid, 21, 29, 32–34, 38, 40, 49, 55, 62–66, 68, 71, 75, 115
Safi 'Ali Shah, 59
Sargon II, 28
Sarmatians, 38
Sasan, 29
Sasanian, 16, 19–20, 23, 27, 29–30, 32, 36, 39–41, 46, 48, 55–57, 68, 115
Saudi Arabia, 112
Scythian, 38
Seistan, 13
Seleucids, 27
Seljuk, 31, 38, 67
Shah 'Abbas II, 76
Shahname, 30, 34, 45
Shaykh al-Islam, 63, 66
Shaykhi sect, 80

Shiite, 15–19, 21, 32–33, 55, 57–60, 64, 80, 84, 111, 115
Shimran, 61
Shiraz, 41, 64, 75, 109
Soviet, 47, 51, 81, 87–88, 101–102, 109–110
Spartans, 21
Sufi, 51, 65
Suhrawardi, 65
Sumka party, 110
Sunni, 15–17, 19, 32, 57, 65, 116
Suren, 41
Swedes, 76, 91
Swiss, 18, 106
Syria, 39

Tabriz, 71, 79–81, 86, 92, 109
Tahmasp, Shah, 63
Tajiks, 13
taqiyeh, 18, 43, 116
Tehran, 18, 42, 60–61, 71, 82, 85, 91, 107
Theophylactus Simocatta, 26
Tiflis, 78
Timurid, 32, 40
Timurtash, 92
Trans-Iranian railroad, 92
Tsar Alexis, 76
Tudeh, 102, 107, 110, 113–114
Turkey, 16–17, 34, 49, 94, 109
Turkomanchai, 78–79
Turks, 16–18, 21, 24, 31–33, 63, 65, 77, 82, 87

Umayyad, 30
United Nations, 112
United States, 51, 78, 82, 97, 102, 110, 112, 114
Urartian, 24, 26
USSR (see Soviet)

Vedas, 24, 45, 53

Wahhabis, 78

Xenophon, 28
Xerxes, 25, 44

Yazd, 71
Yazdegird, 30
Young Turks, 89

Zagros, 14, 16
Zahedi, 113
Zia al-Din, 90
Zoroaster, 30, 53
Zoroastrian, 20, 28, 33, 53–57, 59, 83, 94, 97, 115
Zurvanism, 54